About the Author

Christy Dawn Wilson Beam was born and raised in Abilene, Texas, where she was a teacher for several years. After marrying her high school sweetheart, she left teaching to focus on raising the couple's three girls. Christy and her family now reside in Burleson, Texas, where they are members of Alsbury Baptist Church.

MIRACLES
FROM
HEAVEN

A LITTLE GIRL,

HER JOURNEY TO HEAVEN

AND HER AMAZING STORY OF HEALING

CHRISTY WILSON BEAM

piatkus

PIATKUS

First published in the US in 2015 by Hachette Books, Hachette Book Group
First published in Great Britain in 2015 by Piatkus

13 5 7 9 10 8 6 4 2

A CIP catalogue record for this book
is available from the British Library.

ISBN 978-0-349-40892-7

Typeset in Caslon by M Rules
Printed and bound in Great Britain by
Clays Ltd, St Ives plc

Papers used by Piatkus are from well-managed forests
and other responsible sources.

MIX
Paper from
responsible sources
FSC® C104740

Piatkus
An imprint of
Little, Brown Book Group
100 Victoria Embankment
London EC4Y 0DY

An Hachette UK Company
www.hachette.co.uk

www.piatkus.co.uk

Dedicated to

The One who allowed me to be so many people and so many emotions during this journey with Annabel. The One who was patient as I was filled with anger, sadness, despair, loneliness, and silence. The One who patiently waited and continually carried me when I thought I was alone. The One who mastered everything so delicately like a well-tuned orchestra. The Creator of all good things. The Alpha and Omega, beginning and the end. The One who reigns forever, Yahweh, redeemer, friend!

Prologue

When my husband and I settled down to start a family, we prayed for the ordinary miracles: healthy children, a peaceful home, a newish pickup truck with good AC, and well-timed rain that fell plentifully on the flower beds but never on Friday night football. We expected nothing more breathtaking than a North Texas sunset, nothing more heavenly than growing old together. Our definition of paradise was a secluded plot of land outside Burleson, Texas, a small town just south of the busy Dallas–Fort Worth metropolitan area.

We're church-going people, Kevin and I, people of faith. We've experienced "showers of blessings," as the old gospel song says, "mercy drops falling around us," like when a baby is born after a family has given up hope or strangers cross paths and some tug of the heart tells them they are already friends. We always believed in miracles, in theory. *With God all things are possible*, we're told, and every once in a great,

great while, I'd hear about something that defies odds and brushes fears aside.

Now I'm holding a miracle in my hands.

The nurse hands me a computer printout, two pages listing all the medications my daughter was on last time I brought her to Boston Children's Hospital—the time she told me she wanted to die and be with Jesus in Heaven, where there is no pain.

"Three years ago?" the nurse says, one eyebrow up. "Can that be right?"

That is right. The fact that it's impossible doesn't matter anymore.

"So, Annabel," the nurse says, "looks like you're twelve now."

Anna nods enthusiastically, happy to be twelve, happy to be in Boston, happy to be alive. The nurse directs her to hop up on the scales.

"While I get her vitals, could you please go over these?" the nurse says to me, indicating the printout. "I need you to review for accuracy so I can update the computer. Just mark the ones she's still taking."

My eyes drift down the list.

Prevacid (lansoprazole), a proton pump inhibitor; probiotic supplement; polyethylene glycol; Periactin (cyproheptadine), an antihistamine with additional anticholinergic, antiserotonergic, and local anesthetic agents . . .

It's like looking at the surgical scar on Anna's abdomen, just a pale white line now where she was stitched and reopened and stitched back together again.

Neurontin (gabapentin), an anticonvulsant and analgesic; rifax-imin, a semisynthetic antibiotic based on rifamycin; Augmentin (amoxicillin and clavulanic acid); tramadol hydrochloride for moderate to severe pain . . .

For a moment, the lengthy list blurs in front of my eyes. My God, what her little body went through.

Hyoscyamine, a tropane alkaloid and secondary metabolite; Celexa (citalopram hydrobromide), a selective serotonin reuptake inhibitor . . .

I smile up at the nurse. "She's not on any of these."

"You mean, not any of these?" she says, indicating the first column with a pen.

"No, I mean *these.*" I hold up the two pages in my hands. "She's not taking anything."

"Wow. Okay." She studies the list. "That's really—*wow*—that's . . ."

A miracle.

She doesn't say it, but that's okay. People generally feel more comfortable calling the small things coincidence or serendipity or luck. Doctors use words like *spontaneous remission* to explain away the big-time inexplicable. A while ago, I made the conscious choice to use the M-word. I didn't always see God's hand in the tangled threads of my life, but now I do. He was there in our beginning and every time our world fell apart. He's with us now and into the unknowable future.

Standing in the light of all He's given us, in the light of all that's happened, I can't *not* tell you our story.

Chapter One

The enormous cottonwood tree in the fenced cow pasture beyond our gravel drive was a natural wonder, one of those towering, awesome trees. Take a moment to consider the baking heat and hungry borer beetles, the hard freezes that happen every few years, and the summer tornadoes that routinely whip across central Texas, ragged shirt-tails straggling out from Gulf Coast hurricanes. For a hundred years or more, that cottonwood provided a home for birds, spiders, and squirrels and watched over the sowing and reaping in the surrounding fields. It stood like a sentry as roads cut through the old oaks and houses were built on the rolling farmland.

A balding giant with sparse, heart-shaped leaves, it raised a dome of dry twigs ninety feet in the air. Around the base of the tree, raw knuckles jutted up through the scrub. Thick, sinewy roots anchored it to the ground. The circumference of the trunk was more than any one person could reach around, but three years ago, Kevin and I could have circled it if we joined hands with our daughters—eleven-year-old Abigail, nine-year-old Annabel, and seven-year-old Adelynn—and that's basically how we took on the challenging aspects of our family life. When something came along that was too big to get one's arms around, Kevin and I and the girls only had to reach as far as each other.

About thirty feet up the cottonwood, two massive branches cast outward like open arms. One branch formed a wide bridge to the smaller trees in the shady grove, but the other branch had been broken and lay on the ground. Some mighty rush of wind in some long-ago storm must have wrenched it away and hurled it to the earth. It smashed through the slender boughs below and landed hard, trenching the dirt. High on the broad torso of the tree, a jagged portal was exposed: an opening about four feet high and three feet wide. From the ground below, it looked like the cupped palm of a weathered hand.

The Bible speaks of God preparing a massive fish to swallow Jonah and deliver him on the other side of an angry sea. One might wonder if He began preparing that tree long before any of us were born. One might imagine God whispering into the heart of the cottonwood, *Make a way*. And it did.

Decades came and went, and the tree kept its secret.

In 2002, the year Annabel was born, Kevin and I bought the thirty acres surrounding the cottonwood grove and started building a house. Abbie, Annabel's older sister, was a rambunctious toddler; Adelynn was a prayer we hadn't even thought of yet. I was immersed in the joyful juggling act that happens when "the baby" becomes "the kids." Kevin had just joined a thriving team of vets at Alvarado Veterinary Clinic, where they treated large and small animals—everything from cows to cockapoos and even a kangaroo on one memorable occasion. He has a heart for every creature that comes through the door, and for their owners, but every once in a while, a stray or abused pup would have to come home with him: Trinity, Shadow, wooly white Cypress, clever River, wire-haired Arnold, and dear Jack, part miniature-pinscher and part gladiator, who took it upon himself to stand watch whenever Annabel was sick.

When we moved into our new house, Kevin was thinking *location, location, location.* I was thinking *school district, babysitters, doctor's surgery.* He was thinking about a family business; I was thinking about the business of family—which is why we make a good team. Fast-forward to 2011, and neither of us imagined that our life would revolve around hospital emergency rooms and rare disease specialists. Intubations, CT scans, biopsies, and blood tests—these are things that seem inevitable for our aging grandparents, but for a child? Unthinkable! Kevin and I planned a happy life on our picturesque homestead with our perfect children playing hide-and-seek among the old oaks, swinging from the sturdy branches of the cottonwood, and setting up shop in a solidly built tree fort.

That tall cottonwood in particular was a Swiss Family Robinson adventure waiting to happen: jungle gym, fairy castle, and wild animal safari all in one. Abbie and a friend had climbed up one of the smaller neighboring trees to that natural bridge, where they sat and surveyed the world and imagined all sorts of things and returned with a lovely little bird's nest that had been left empty as winter came on. This amazing treasure fascinated Annabel and Adelynn, but Adelynn was too small to shinny up the cottonwood trees, and Annabel wasn't feeling well enough to go out and play.

"It could be the meds giving her migraine headaches," I said to Kevin, "but if we take her off any of that, do we risk another obstruction in her intestine?"

"Let's not borrow trouble," he said. "She has her regular follow-up this week in Boston. If there's anything going on, they'll nail it."

Flying out of Dallas–Fort Worth, Anna and I left the city and manicured suburbs far below. The busy traffic turned to a crawling anthill. The farms and oil fields spread out like a faded patchwork quilt. Annabel rested her forehead against the airplane window and watched it all disappear below the clouds, her thoughts far away, her eyes hazy with the familiar pain of a lingering migraine. She'd made this trip enough times to know she could charm an extra Sprite from the flight attendants with her sweet nature and ready smile. She also knew what lay ahead of her at Children's Hospital in Boston: days of poking and prodding, blood tests and body scans, invasive tests that left her wrung out and frustrated.

"It's just for the day," I reminded her. "We'll be home before you know it, and then, just like *that*"—I snapped my fingers—"it'll be Christmas."

Immediately on board for the positive spin, Annabel nodded happily and lifted my arm up and around her shoulders, and I drifted my thumb across her collarbone near the site where a PICC line—a peripherally inserted central catheter—had been placed to deliver parenteral nutrition directly to her bloodstream during the miserable episodes when pseudo-obstruction motility disorder made it impossible for her little body to process food or even water in the normal way. In simple terms, pseudo-obstruction motility disorder is when things don't move normally from point A to point B in the intestines. Sometimes this is nerve related and sometimes it's muscle related; Annabel's specific issue affected her nerves' ability to "fire" synchronically. Flare-ups often look and act very similar to intestinal obstruction. Hence the name *pseudo-obstruction*.

For four years, we'd been dealing with the brutal realities behind all that clinical vocabulary. We'd fought long and hard, first to get to that devastating diagnosis, then to find some kind of hope and meaningful help for our Anna. We finally found our way to Dr. Samuel Nurko, director of the Center for Motility and Functional Gastrointestinal Disorders at Boston Children's Hospital and an associate professor of pediatrics at Harvard Medical School. He's recognized as one of the world's leading experts on pseudo-obstruction motility disorder, but Anna and his other patients love him for his quick, wide smile and his bright Elmo neckties. He was a life raft. We clung to him, though the expenses of the treatment and travel were bleeding us dry. This particular trip had been financed by the sale of Kevin's upmarket, fitted-out, *Look, Ma, I'm a Texas animal doctor!* pickup truck, which he'd paid off with great pride a few years earlier.

Quality of life is difficult to maintain for children with this chronic and life-threatening disorder; we were desperate for anything to ease Anna's pain and make it possible for her to lead some semblance of a normal life. Dr. Nurko was one of just a few doctors in the United States who were able to prescribe cisapride, a drug that had been officially taken off the market because of possible damage to the heart and liver. The regular trips to Boston were an imperative part of the balancing act between various clinical risks and silver linings.

Kevin can get into his surgical scrubs and see the science behind it all. I tend to take it more personally. As a mother, how could I not? I mean, think about the priorities of caring for an infant, when you're focused on the basic necessities of life. You fuss about what goes in, and you monitor what comes out; these are the basic components of your baby's well-being. In order to live, your body has to properly process three things: air, blood, and food. Two outta three ain't gonna cut it. And while major malfunction of the first two would kill you with swift mercy, major malfunction of that third one is a dragging agony.

When your body gets seriously hung up on some failure in the food-processing department, any medical help available to you is humiliating at best, and at worst, it's an inconceivable assault on your physical and emotional well-being. Annabel had gone a long way toward the latter end of that spectrum. This damnable dragon bit right into the middle of her, and it was relentless, and Kevin and I couldn't slay that dragon for her, and it broke our hearts.

Through all the pain and invasive procedures, the struggles keeping up in school and being left behind while her sisters thrived, Annabel had displayed a sort of chin-up acceptance I can only describe as amazing grace. During the first two years or so, receiving bad news and setbacks one after the other, Kevin and I developed a thick skin, receiving the latest round of test results like a pair of skeptical armadillos. Annabel, on the other hand, was optimistic about new treatment protocols and philosophical about failed ones. She endured the needles, tubes, and electrodes stoically and did her best to cooperate like a model patient 99 percent of the time. She radiated peace and joy, which was a magnet for loving kindness. We were surrounded by a tight circle of friends and family who baked and prayed and went out of their way for us, stepping up at a moment's notice to take care of Abbie and Adelynn.

At the airport in Boston, we were greeted by our good friends, Beth and Steve Harris, who never let us get off the airplane and face the city alone. We originally connected with them through the wife of the pastor who married Kevin and me. She'd been praying for our family, for Anna's struggles, and when she heard we were headed for Boston, she reached out to her good friends, Beth and Steve, who never once let us arrive at the airport without someone to greet us and give us a ride to our hotel.

Beth swept Annabel into her arms, and we headed for Passenger Pickup.

"Are you ready for Christmas?" Beth asked.

"We're keeping it low-key this year," I said. "Family stuff."

This was not as low-key as it sounds, of course. Beam family holidays are a whole lot of "over the river and through the woods": pre-Christmas with my parents (Maw Maw and Paw Paw) in Wichita Falls, Christmas Eve with Kevin's parents (Gran Jan and P Paw) in Houston, and New Year's Eve with Kevin's nonny (that's "grandma" if you're north of the Mason–Dixon Line) at her condo by the sea in Corpus Christi.

"Well, that sounds like a blast, doesn't it?" said Beth.

"It is absolutely a blast," Annabel declared. She deftly navigated the escalator with her little rolling bag, a seasoned traveler.

I caught her elbow and said, "Anna, sweetie, stop a sec and get your coat on before we go outside."

She was wearing a pink T-shirt with a sparkly butterfly and a short-sleeved jersey jacket that zipped up the front—her favorite fashion statement at that moment—which was perfect for a sunny December day in Dallas–Fort Worth but not so much for Boston. As she paused to pull on her warm parka, I noticed that during the flight, the little butterfly shirt had gotten tighter over her distended tummy. An uneasy feeling trickled down the back of my neck.

We arrived at the car and exchanged another round of warm hugs with Steve.

"How long are you here?" he asked. "Will you have time to go out to dinner with us?" Steve and Beth were perfect dinner companions, familiar with the limited menu that might work for Anna when she was able to eat solid foods.

"Just overnight this time," I said. "Routine checkup, blood work, and ECG to make sure the meds aren't affecting her heart. Done and dusted." I made a breezy gesture with my hand. "In one door and out the other."

I wasn't allowing any other possibility to cast a shadow on us. Not this time, because that was the plan, and Kevin and the girls were waiting for us to come home, and *c'mon, Lord, it's Christmas!*

Guess our pet dragon didn't get that memo.

"Annabel needs to be admitted," I was told the next morning. "We don't like what we're seeing. We need to see what's going on in the digestive tract. She's pale, very distended, and the indigenous migraine is another troubling issue."

"I understand the need for further testing," I said carefully. "The thing is, she's been in the hospital a lot in the last two years—*a lot*—and she's a trouper, but she'll be devastated. And last week, she was like her normal self—what is normal for her, I mean. As good as it gets. She had the chronic pain, but she was eating and drinking, and her system seemed to be working relatively well. This was supposed to be a routine checkup. Please, if you treat the acute issue, do something about the pain and then let her go; we can follow up with Dr. Siddiqui in Austin. He was trained up by Dr. Nurko. They work very closely together. And right close to home we have our wonderful pediatrician, Dr. Moses—he's been caring for Anna since she was a baby."

I tried hard not to sound like I was begging. But I was begging. Begging this doctor, begging God—I'd have even begged Santa if it would have done any good.

"They're admitting her," I told Kevin on the phone that night. I felt his heavy sigh on the other end of the line. He knew the drill as well as I did, and so did Annabel. She'd start out NPO—*non per os*—which means nothing to eat or drink. IVs were started to rehydrate her and allow her intestines to rest. Next would come the preparations for the invasive upper and lower gastrointestinal testing, the barium enema and colonoscopy, to make sure we weren't heading for another dangerous obstruction.

"What's her pain level?" Kevin asked.

"She says six or seven, but you know what a stoic she is. She always understates it."

"How's her spirit?"

"Not good," I said. "I've never seen her like this, Kevin. She's just staring at the TV, won't get up to look out the window or go to the playroom, won't talk to anyone . . ."

"Mommy," Annabel whimpered, "can I get a heat pack for my stomach?"

"Sure, sweet girl." I handed her my cell phone. "Here, talk to Daddy while I run down the hall to the nurses' station and get it. That'll be faster than ringing the buzzer."

By the time I came back with the heat pack, her daddy had her giggling a little. She was still subdued, for Annabel, but my heart grasped at the sound of her soft laughter. I got her set up with the heat pack, and she handed me my phone.

"I should let you go," I told Kevin. "You've got an early morning at work."

"It'll be okay, babe," Kevin said, but I could tell he didn't believe that any more than I did. "I love you, Christy."

"I love you too."

"Tell Anna I love her. I told her already, but . . . you know. Tell her again."

"I will," I said. "Tell Abbie and Adelynn I miss them something awful."

"They miss you too."

"Tell them to brush their teeth. And floss. And tell Abbie to pry her nose out of her book and help you with supper."

"I got it covered. Don't worry about it."

We said "I love you" once more. Maybe more than once more. I clicked off the phone, dimmed the lights, kicked off my shoes, and lay down on Anna's bed, spooning her, gathering her small, warm body against my belly as if I could still shelter and protect her there.

"The halls are all decorated with a million twinkling Christmas lights," I said, stroking her hair away from her forehead. "After you take a nap, we'll go for a walk."

"I don't feel like it." She sounded so hollowed out and sad.

"Oh, c'mon now. Deck the halls, right? This place—they got halls for days, I'm here to tell ya."

"No, thank you."

"Should we see if they have the Disney Channel? Maybe that show with Selena Gomez is on. Or I could read to you till you fall asleep. Would you like that?"

"No."

"Annabel ... my sweet girl ..."

I felt her breath catch in her chest, and for the first time in her long, arduous journey, she was overtaken with a deep, inconsolable weeping. An ocean of sorrow seemed to swallow her up in wave upon wave of bitter tears. My whole soul wept with her, but I bit back my own tears, trying to give her something solid to hold on to, encouraging her to breathe, pressing kisses to the crown of her head, smoothing my hand over the heat pack on the hard swell of her tummy. I clenched my jaw in fervent, silent prayer: *Please, Lord, please, let me take the pain. I'll take it for her, Lord. I'll do anything if you'll please, please, just let me take it. I beg you, I beg you, have mercy ...*

She cried for a long time, wracking sobs broken with genuinely baffled questions: *Why am I like this? Why can't I be like my sisters? How can this keep happening when so many people with so much faith have held me up in prayer so many times?* I had no answers for her. I'd been asking the same questions!

Her weeping finally settled into an exhausted, hicuppy inhaling and exhaling. She seemed to let go of the day, her whole body limp and feverish; the crackling electric energy that makes her Annabel seemed to dissipate with each quiet sigh. I lay listening to the quiet activity at the nurses' station down the hall, the soft *pip pip* of the IV by the bed. I thought Annabel had fallen asleep.

"Mommy ... I just want to die and go to Heaven and be with Jesus where there's no pain."

A ripple of cold shock went through me.

"Annabel ..." I groped for the right response. "If you ...

if you went to Heaven, then you wouldn't be with me and Daddy. There'd be a big hole in my soul. I would be so sad."

"No, Mommy," she said without missing a beat, "you would kill yourself and go with me."

"*Anna . . .*" No words came.

The statement was so blunt, so matter-of-fact and without hesitation, such a dark sentiment from such a bright spirit. Sickened, stunned with sadness, I realized: She'd been thinking about it, pragmatically considering all the angles. She had it all figured out.

When Annabel fell asleep, I crept out into the hall and called Kevin.

"Physically, she's no worse than she's been in the past," I told him, "but mentally she's in a place that really scares me."

Thinking back on it now, I don't know why I was so blindsided by her wish—her prayer—to go and be with God. Annabel is a realist whose middle name is Faith. Why wouldn't she want to be done with this long, grueling fight? I was the one who told her about God and Jesus and the unclouded day of Heaven. I knew she would be safe there, free from pain and forever joyful with her savior, but with my whole selfish heart, I wanted her with me. With my whole soul, I willed her to hang on.

Please, God, please, don't do this. Oh, Jesus, give her the strength to go on.

Over the next few days, physical therapists were sent in to badger her out of bed, and a child psychologist was sent in to encourage her to talk about her feelings. After the NPO period, when they were satisfied that there was no obstruction and her digestive tract was being coaxed into action again, the nurses and I wheedled and pleaded with her to eat and drink, but she continued to rely on the IV as her sole source of nutrition and hydration. She was capable of moving, eating, drinking, playing—she could have gotten out of bed; she chose not to. She usually loved to have Beth, who was warm and stylish and funny, come over and hang out so I could pop back to the hotel and grab a shower. Now Anna just wanted to nap, and she wanted me to stay right there with her while she slept.

"Do you know how many people are praying for you today?" I said to her each morning. "A whole lot. Maw Maw and her whole Sunday school class in Wichita Falls are praying for you. Paw Paw and all the other deacons at the church are praying for you. Gran Jan and P Paw and Nonny and all our friends and family ..."

I stroked her head, reciting that litany of love, hoping she'd feel their prayers around her like a great fortress.

Dr. Nurko had been called out of town on a family emergency, so instead of sitting with our trusted champion in the familiar clutter of the hospital playroom, I sat at the end of a conference table facing the whole medical rugby team. Charts and scans mapping the long physical siege were spread out in front of them. This was the first time Anna's spirit had seriously flagged, and now her mental state was as tenuous and terrifying as the lurking disorder in her intestines.

"We're very concerned," someone said.

Nods all around with a grimly echoed, "Very concerned."

I longed for the solid comfort of Kevin's unflappable presence at my side. From the beginning, I was the Mama Bear in Chief. I had no trouble hassling and haranguing on Annabel's behalf, but Kevin knew the right questions to ask. He spoke the language of diagnostics and had the credentials that changed their tone of voice. They'd call me "Mom" and give me a tolerant smile; they'd call Kevin "Doctor" and give him answers.

A variety of strategies were put forward, including the idea that we should cut back on her cisapride dosage and add an antidepressant to the mix, but before we had a chance to see if that was working, the best possible thing happened.

That morning, after Kevin and I had been talking, he clicked off his phone, strode to the bottom of the stairs, and called, "Abigail! Get bags together for you and Adelynn."

She knew the procedure; she and Adelynn were frequently roused from their beds or fetched from school and told they were being farmed out to friends or family while Kevin and I took Annabel to the ER. Within minutes, she had herself and her little sister packed and ready to roll. They headed out to the rattletrap diesel truck Kevin had borrowed from the veterinary clinic. It was a noisy replacement for the sleek Docmobile he'd worked so hard for, but he was grateful to have wheels.

"Where are we going?" Abbie asked as they climbed into the cab.

"Boston."

He grimly steered for the airport an hour away, and while

15

they were driving, Abbie fished one credit card after another from his wallet and read him the numbers on the back so he could call and plead with them to extend him enough to buy plane tickets for himself and the girls. We'll never truly know what it took for him to do that. Kevin took great pride in his self-reliance. He'd worked his way through school, studied hard, achieved high results; he'd built a solid career, making a good living and a good life for me and the girls. He was committed to teaching them by example about the work ethic, integrity, and self-reliance. He's just that salt-of-the-earth kind of guy. But he couldn't take the thought of what was happening in Boston, so far away, not being able to help Annabel.

It was pretty humbling, he told me later, to get in that ramshackle loaned pickup with ten dollars in his pocket and hold that cell phone to his head, trying to beg, borrow, and wangle an allowance from strangers while his daughter listened, wide-eyed, wanting to help him. Having her witness that made it a thousand times worse. But Abbie is an old soul, I told him; she's wise enough to know there is no man stronger than the man who's willing to lay down his pride for his family. Kevin finally got a tentative go-ahead from a customer rep at one of the card companies. She couldn't actually raise the limit, but she told him to try it.

"You never know," she said. "It might go through."

Thank God for small favors, as the saying goes.

Late that night, Annabel was lying in her hospital bed, awake but uninterested in the television that droned in the corner. When Kevin and the girls burst through the door of her hospital room, she was fourteen kinds of flabbergasted. The look on her face (and on mine, I'll bet!) was priceless. Kevin gathered her into his arms while Abbie and Adelynn came running and hung on to me like koalas climbing a tree.

"Waaaaait a minute." Annabel blinked, trying to process it. "I'm in *Boston*. What are you doing here?"

"We came to see you!" Abigail and Adelynn laughed and clambered onto the bed to show her the get-well pictures they'd made for her on the plane. "We want you to get better!"

Kevin and I looked at each other over the tops of their honey-colored heads. And then Abigail—always Instigator at Large in the Beam sisters posse—accomplished in thirty seconds flat what the doctors, nurses, therapists, and I hadn't been able to do all week.

"Show us the playroom, Anna," she said. "Do they have one here?"

"Yeah, but I don't feel like—"

"*Let's go.*" Abbie was having none of that. "C'mon!"

And just like that, Annabel was out of bed, wielding the IV pole like an old pro, and headed out the door, all of us following like a Mardi Gras parade. It was after 11:00 p.m., but the nurses were so thrilled to see a spark of life in her, they opened the playroom and let the Beam sisters take charge of the place, all over each other, shrill and giggling. Annabel was too weak for any degree of physical rowdiness, but Abbie and Adelynn instinctively "brought the mountain to Mohammad," creating a game that incorporated the cumbersome IV apparatus and reimagined all the bright-colored furnishings in the little playroom.

"Abbie," said Annabel, "will you do the witch skit?"

Adelynn was instantly on her side. "Yes! Abbie, do the witch skit! Please, please, please?"

The command performance of Abbie's one-girl show began as it did every time Anna was in the hospital, with Abbie playing the sweet little maid girl who was for some reason consigned to serve a terrible witch, also played by Abbie, who for some unspecified reason intended to do the maid girl harm. But everything the witch tried to do went off the rails in some spectacular slapstick way. She'd trip over her broom. Her kettle would boil over. An owl would get snaggled in her hair. While Kevin and I retreated to the corner to discuss "the yucky stuff," the poor witch met with one disaster after another, and Annabel and Adelynn laughed themselves practically inside out.

Since there was more "yuck" than usual this time, I finally told the girls they could go and look at the massive Christmas tree in the lobby.

"Abbie's in charge, all right? Adelynn, I mean it. You do as Abbie says. Quiet in the hallway. Don't bother the nurses. Abbie, take my cell phone and call Daddy's phone every ten minutes to check in, okay?"

Annabel wilted a little. "Mommy, I don't feel good. I just want to lie down."

"Anna, it's an adventure," Abbie said. "Plus you'll feel better if you walk a little. We'll pretend we're in a movie that's in *slooooooooooww mmmmmoooooshhhhhhuuuuunnnnnn*!"

So now it was a game, and Annabel couldn't resist. I smiled at Abbie over her head and whispered, "You're brilliant!"

As they oozed down the hallway, giggling and swimming through the thick air, I leaned on the wall.

"Oh, babe . . ." I said, not knowing where to begin.

He set his jaw square, but emotion welled in his eyes.

"I came to take my family home," he said.

I stepped into the arms of this man I love, the only home I'd ever need.

Chapter Two

The next morning, we were determined to convince the doctor that Annabel was better off out of the hospital, but it was really Annabel who persuaded him with an unmistakable new spark of life. He released her with the understanding that we needed to watch her closely to make sure the change in meds didn't bring on any unwelcome side effects. While it would mean charging more on our credit cards with our fingers crossed, we agreed to stay in Boston for the weekend so we'd be able to rush her back to the hospital if things went awry. We would stay at the hotel next door, the Inn at Longwood Medical, and we scheduled a follow-up with Dr. Anees Siddiqui, Dr. Nurko's protégé in Austin, to rebalance her meds if necessary.

Despite the circumstances—or maybe because of them—we had a wonderful family weekend. During the bright winter days, we walked the Freedom Trail, visited the Children's Museum, and strolled through the aquarium. At night, we took in the spectacular Christmas lights all over the city and snuggled together with pillows and blankets in front of the hotel room TV. The city was full of carols and bells and busy good cheer, and the girls were swept up in sheer kid-at-Christmastime delight. For three Southern sisters, Boston in mid-December was an up-north winter wonderland. Annabel was weak; she spent most of the time riding on her daddy's shoulders and had to work at eating and drinking, but her spirit seemed to rebound. And so did mine. Every time we all burst out laughing at something, which happens a lot in our family, I felt a jolt of pure joy.

Monday morning, Kevin and I spoke with the doctor, but we were reluctant to bring Annabel back to the hospital to see him. Physically, she was no worse—pale, with her usual distention and chronic pain—and her emotional state seemed so fragile. We felt that we'd grabbed her back from the brink and didn't want to force her that close to the edge again. Kevin was plenty capable of monitoring her vitals, and I was plenty familiar with the warning signs; we decided to take her home with plans to follow up with the specialist in Austin.

Annabel's good pal Angela, who worked as a waitress in the hotel restaurant, popped by to visit us before we headed home on Tuesday. Annabel had a special Christmas gift for her: a bracelet woven from pipe cleaners.

"I made this for you so you won't forget me," Annabel said, slipping it over Angela's hand. "Purple, because that's your favorite color, and pink, because that's my favorite color. And white is for peace."

Anna threw her arms around Angela and hugged her tight. In Angela's eyes, I could see the same questions that weighed on me. Later, she e-mailed me: "For the first time in my life, I was truly at a loss for words. Why would she say that to me? How could I ever forget her? I didn't ask her. I was so afraid of her answers."

A few weeks after we got home, Kevin's parents—Gran Jan and P Paw to the girls—hosted the quintessential idyllic Christmas for the whole family at their home in Houston.

I joined the major league of motherhood when I married into the clan with Gran Jan and her mother, Nonny, who is approaching ninety and still busting into super-nonny mode anytime her family needs her, which we have on several difficult occasions. After Nonny moved to Corpus, the holidays were spread out with Christmas Eve and Christmas Day at Gran Jan and P Paw's and New Year's at Nonny's.

There's an old church song that likens Heaven to a family reunion, and it certainly felt that way when we arrived on Christmas Eve, hugging and greeting everyone. Kevin's big brother Eric was there with his wife, Melissa, and their kids Braiden (already a dude at thirteen), Brooke (a perfectly timed ten, right between Abbie and Anna), and Bennett (only five, but working it). Then came our crew, followed by Kevin's little sister Corrie with her husband, Mark, and their two little girls, toddler Landrie and baby Tatum.

The girls dumped their backpacks and were out the door in about thirty seconds flat, headed for the backyard where

Braiden and Brooke were already climbing in the huge old oak tree.

"Listen, sisters," I called sharply, and when they turned to me, I struggled with a mouthful of the standard caveats: *Be careful! Slow down! Not too high!*

"Mom," they groaned in unison. Annabel folded her arms, reading my mind.

Kevin and I resolved early on that we would never treat Annabel like the poor little sick girl; she was anything but that. All three of our girls are rough-and-tumble tomboys, country kids who climb trees and jump over puddles and go rolling over the cattle grid in an old tractor tire, which means we present ourselves at the local ER for the occasional broken bone or tetanus shot. That day at Gran Jan's, the occasional broken bone or tetanus shot that comes with being a happily unstoppable force of nature was far less frightening to me than seeing Anna's crumpled spirit in that hospital bed in Boston. She was not foolish or reckless by nature, she had Abbie looking out for her, and she'd had enough of people hovering and fussing and telling her she couldn't do things.

"Y'all have fun," I said.

They bounded off like three golden retrievers, and I went inside to scope out a strategic spot where I could spy on them through the window. Abbie was the first one to the tree, but it didn't take Anna long to catch up, and within moments, she was up into the branches, determined to go higher and be braver than anyone else.

"They'll be fine," Corrie said, looking over my shoulder.

Another mind reader. "Goodness, Anna's quite a little monkey, isn't she?"

"She has absolutely no fear," I said. "I have to be scared enough for both of us."

The cousin crew ran themselves ragged until dusk—climbing, leaping, swinging, laughing—inhabiting the branches of the old oak like a chattering flock of crows. Just about the time the streetlights came on, they trooped in for hot chocolate and cookies.

The house was decorated to the nines, but very kid friendly. There's always a Christmas village out, and the kids are allowed to zoom Matchbox cars in and out of the large houses. A little row of Hallmark houses lines the mantel where we hang stockings, which were handmade by Nonny, good and stretchy for maximum stuffing and overstuffing. The evergreen tree, fresh-cut and fragrant, was heavy with memento ornaments and had to be set up on an elevated stand to accommodate all the presents pouring out from underneath. Of course, being an eleven-year-old, Abbie was wise to the real deal, but Annabel and Adelynn were still willing to be thrilled and amazed at how Santa had gotten the memo that our family would be at Gran Jan and P Paw's for Christmas and could he please drop by with their toys, books, and new clothes.

The huge room where we open presents is decorated with antique farm equipment, including a well-used horse-drawn plow, from the old Beam family farm in Indiana. Every corner is filled with memories of Mimi, P Paw's mom, and the farm; the girls had a blast visiting her there, as Kevin always did when he was a growing up, but they really got to know her after she moved to an assisted-living apartment near Kevin's parents in Houston. We loved to hear Mimi sing at the piano—all the old church songs; she played by heart and had a beautiful voice.

We missed her that Christmas; she'd been gone barely a year.

Looking at home movies of that Christmas, I have to smile at how Abbie is traipsing around with Landrie on her hip, so ready to babysit, even though I wasn't quite ready to let her. Adelynn rips into her Christmas stocking, providing a hilarious running commentary on every item. Annabel is subdued but still a kid on Christmas morning, and it's heartbreaking to see her approach the camera with her stocking to unload her sweets while the other kids in the background are already devouring theirs.

Kevin, who's holding the camera, says, "Maybe you can ask Mommy if you can have just one."

"That's okay," she says. "It's not worth getting sick on Christmas. You can have these, Daddy."

"Okay, I'll eat the chocolate," Kevin says. "I'll make that sacrifice for you, baby girl."

We all laugh, and I tell her, "You can have a few mints, Anna." And she's happy with that.

That evening, the car radios and cool air were filled with carols. Hundreds of homes in the neighborhood participate in their annual Night of Lights. Texans are not known for understatement; these folks go all out with giant inflatable snowmen, freestanding plywood reindeer, and blow mold plastic Candylands. There are traditional nativity scenes, cowboy-themed nativity scenes, African American nativity scenes, Stars of David, Stars of Bethlehem, Lone Stars, and lights of every shape and color and style, including the very popular little red Tex-Mex chili peppers, flashing and blinking and blazing everywhere. Every year, thousands of visitors are welcome to drive slowly up and down the cul-de-sacs, minding the many pedestrians and taking in the spirit of the season. Our girls love cruising those Christmas lights every year, backseat windows open, necks craning to see the stars and fully loaded sleighs mounted on the rooftops.

I sat in the middle of the front seat, my head on Kevin's shoulder, listening to the girls singing along with the radio, and I had to smile, hearing an echo of Mimi's singing in their clear soprano voices.

Sleep in heavenly peace . . .

When I was a little girl, my daddy was a church deacon and my mama sang in the choir. I remember her practicing every year to be part of the Living Christmas Tree. The whole choir stood on platforms that formed a big Christmas tree with every singing soul as a beautiful ornament. Anna and her sisters had been hearing the traditional carols all their lives—along with the old-school Christmas story from Luke 2. I love the part where it says that Mary, the mother of Jesus, looked back on all that happened during her first year of motherhood, the harrowing days of hardship and faith, the terrifying and the miraculous.

She gathered all these things and pondered them in her heart, Luke says.

In the glow of the Christmas lights, I thought about Boston. Anna's despair. Kevin's heroic leap of faith. Precious gifts made with love and received with joy. To be here now, surrounded by family, was the greatest gift I could imagine, but I was just as happy to walk through the door of our own house.

Our boisterous welcoming committee met us at the door, wagging and barking, led by Cypress, Anna's big white goldendoodle. A few years earlier, Kevin had done some surgery for a doodle rescue organization. The head of the organization was moved when she heard how Anna was struggling with her health; as a thank-you for Kevin's work, she offered her the pick of a recently rescued litter of pups. She chose a clumsy, delightful male named Haus because he was huge, but she renamed him Cypress to go with the river-themed names of our other dogs. Cypress was beside himself with joy when Anna walked in the door. She'd been away too much for his taste, and over the next few days, he hardly let her out of his sight.

Thank God for that week between Christmas and New Year's. We always need that time to jog off Gran Jan's amazing Southern cooking and prepare for the sumptuous New Year's Eve spread featuring Nonny's baked goods. Meanwhile, laundry was piled a mile high. The mailbox was jammed with medical bills and credit card statements. Though I hadn't done as much as I usually do to decorate the house for Christmas, I'd done enough to make the undoing of it a daunting chore in itself. Most important, I wanted the girls to have a moment to enjoy the school break before we had to take Anna to Austin for her follow-up appointment with Dr. Siddiqui, when we might face the possibility of another hospital siege.

The first few days after Christmas, Annabel was visibly wiped out. All that fun had taken a toll on her energy. She'd done fairly well with the small quantity of holiday treats she was allowed, but her tummy was still distended, and she asked for pain meds while she lay in front of the TV with the heat pack. She didn't seem depressed, but she was quiet. Sometimes it was her usual stoic quiet. Other times it was a resounding, thoughtful sort of quiet that troubled me, and as if he sensed it, too, Cypress nuzzled and napped close to her side.

December 30, 2011, was bright and balmy, the sort of winter day we keep in mind when summers become unbearable, about 67°F as the late afternoon shadows stretched out around the cottonwood grove. Abigail and Adelynn had been outside playing most of the day. Abigail is a bookworm, but it does the opposite of make her a couch potato. Instead, all those stories bouncing around in her head spur her imagination, and she's always recruiting her sisters to populate some faraway mermaid reef or space station or unicorn rodeo. She'd been patiently but persistently nudging Anna to come out and play since we got home from Houston, so I was pleasantly surprised when Annabel popped her head into the laundry room to tell me, "I'm going out with Abbie and Adelynn."

"Oh? Okay. Good." I nodded and smiled but didn't want her to feel like I was making a big deal out of it. She was wearing her trusty zip-up T-shirt with the sparkly butterfly.

I tugged the short sleeve and asked, "Will you be warm enough?"

She folded her arms and gave me the *puh-leeeeeze, do I look like a baby?* look. I didn't even bother suggesting shoes. Annabel was born barefoot and remains determined to stay that way 95 percent of the time. Abbie's and Adelynn's shoes had been left by the door too. It was a barefoot sort of day outside.

"Y'all be careful," I said. "Supper in a little while."

She dashed out the door, her shoulder-length hair flying every which way, Cypress bounding after her. Before I returned to the housekeeping tasks at hand, I closed my eyes and breathed a sincere, "Thank you, God." Seeing one's kid dash out the door to play might not seem like a miracle to everybody, but it was miracle for me.

For that moment.

In the years that followed, I asked Kevin and the girls and a number of other people to write down what they recalled about the six hours that came after that. I put it all together like puzzle pieces with everything I knew then about my girls and everything I learned about the tree and everything I believe about God. I did what Mary did. I gathered. I pondered. That's how I'm able to tell you this story now. Because from my perspective, those six hours still feel like a marbled wall of fervent prayer and raw terror.

The leaves in the cottonwood grove whispered in the breeze high over Adelynn's head. She paced on top of the fallen branch as if it were a balance beam, put off and pouting because she was too small to climb up in the tree, and Abbie and Anna were not about to come down. Bracing themselves between two tree trunks, they'd shinnied up, inching higher, higher, high enough to grasp and hoist themselves onto that accommodating branch—the one that formed the natural bridge to the smaller trees—where Abbie and her friend had found the abandoned birds' nest.

There'd been some speculation around the dinner table at the time about what might be inside the yawning grotto high on the side of the tree trunk.

"Baby raccoons, maybe."

"Or squirrels."

"No, a honeycomb! Like in *Winnie-the-Pooh*."

"If there's honey, there'd be a million bees too."

The branch just below the open cavity was as broad as a park bench and didn't feel precarious at all. It just felt wonderfully skyscraper high, like being on the third-floor balcony at Nonny's condo, but with your own grassy pasture below and your own house just on the other side of the cattle grid. The girls weren't afraid of falling; they fully expected to go down the same way they went up. So they sat for a long while, taking in the last of the sunshine, discussing all sorts of things. I didn't push them to confide in me about the particulars of their private conversation, but I would have loved to be a little squirrel up there in the branches, eavesdropping on these two sweet sisters swinging their feet and talking about life.

When the dry branch groaned beneath them, they froze for a moment, looking at each other with wide eyes and slightly open mouths, neither one of them daring to take a breath. They looked down at the soft brown grass thirty feet below. Suddenly it looked prickly and pocked with jagged rocks, littered with sharp sticks and jutting twigs.

"It's okay," said Abbie. "When I was up here with—"

The branch shifted with an abrupt crack, and the girls screamed.

"*Abbie!*"

"Annabel. Don't. Move."

"We need to get down. Abbie, I want to get down."

Far below their feet, Cypress paced and whined. Adelynn looked up at them and called out, "What's the matter with you? When are y'all coming down?"

Abbie swallowed and called down to her, "Don't be scared, Adelynn. We're coming down. Right now. We're coming down. We're okay. Anna, can you . . ."

"I think so."

They carefully got to their feet. The branch seemed to exhale an agonized sigh. A moment before, they were sitting on a castle bridge. Now it felt brittle and tilted, and that far end of the bridge seemed very, very far away.

"Anna, you have to go back that way." Abbie pointed to the slender tree behind her. "Let me get around you and get my weight off the branch. I'll go down over there." She nodded in the direction of the craggy tree trunk. "Just scooch over so I can get around you. Go, Anna. Move over by the trunk where it's safer. I'm right behind you."

They inched toward the gaping wound left by the fallen branch.

"Okay," said Abbie, "step into the cave for a sec so I can get around you."

32

"No." Annabel shook her head. "I don't want to."

"Annabel, just do it. It's only for a second. I need to get on that side, and then I'll help you get down."

"Abbie, no! I don't want to!"

Another sharp crack. Another arthritic sigh.

"*Annabel! Just go! Go now!*"

"I don't want to. Abbie ... I don't like this," Anna whimpered, genuinely afraid now, but she set one foot on the jagged edge of the opening. Bits of bark and rotted wood broke away when she put weight on it. She grasped the side of the opening, peering inside. The sun was close to the horizon now. She could see nothing but deep shadows in the musty grotto.

"Anna, *move*. Hurry," Abbie said, inching toward the tree trunk.

"How deep is it?"

"I don't know, maybe a foot? How deep does it look?"

"A foot ... I guess ..."

"Anna, come on! Just go."

Anna gingerly stepped her other foot onto the edge, and it instantly gave way. She grasped at the other side with her hands. Leaning across the gaping hole, fighting to hold herself up, she felt the ledge crumbling beneath her feet, felt the strength sifting from her arms.

Annabel managed to hold herself there for a moment. But in that moment, she realized there was nothing but darkness below her. And the next moment, she was gone.

Chapter Three

This is what I know now about the cottonwood tree: It is related to the aspen and poplar, with quaking leaves that turn brilliant gold in autumn. It is one of the largest trees native to North America, but its seeds are only half as wide as the head of a pin. The female cottonwood has blossoms with fluffy white tufts that give the tree its name. It is armored with thick, corklike bark, able to withstand prairie fires, brutal drought, and bitter cold. So the cottonwood stands strong, green and growing, even as age and disease decay the heartwood deep inside the limbs and trunk. The fallen branch and the open wound, we later learned, were the signs.

As Annabel dropped away into the darkness, the tree revealed its secret at last: From the jagged grotto to the gnarled roots thirty feet below, it was hollow.

She says she hit her head three times on the way down, and this is consistent with the findings of an MRI scan. With the facts in front of me now, I see it all with sickening clarity.

Sometimes at night, it replays in my head, a dark twist on Alice tumbling down the rabbit hole.

Annabel plummeted headfirst down the long vertical corridor, flailing for any kind of handhold. The first of the blunt blows to her head might have happened as she pitched forward or at some point as her body hurtled past misshapen walls and jutting knots. The second may have been her skull glancing off a knotty ledge that protruded eight inches or so inside the tree roughly five feet from the bottom. The third—oh, God, it's hard to think about—happened when she hit the ground.

Her little body folded on impact. Fragments of bark, rotting wood, and dry moss rained down in her wake. Heaped in a distorted fetal position, Annabel lay at the bottom of the black, airless shaft.

"Anna? Anna, are you okay?"

High on the unstable cottonwood branch, Abbie inched forward until she was able to clutch the side of the opening where Annabel had disappeared.

"What's wrong?" Adelynn called from below. "What happened?"

"Annabel, are you stuck?"

Leaning forward as far as she dared, Abbie peeped over the crumbled edge into the cavity. She could see that it was more than a few feet deep, but the sun was low on the horizon now; she could see only shadows inside the tree.

"Anna? Anna, are you okay?" Abbie called. "Annabel? *Anna*. You better not be messing with me."

The only answer was the soft murmur of the cottonwood leaves.

Abbie squeezed her eyes shut. *Think. Think. Think.*

Scrambling across the bridge branch, she swung down through the branches, dropped to the grass, and ran. She pounded across the pasture toward the house, leaped the cattle grid, and rounded the drive. I don't think she even paused at the back door. Instead of coming in to get me, she ducked into the garage, snatched a headlamp flashlight from Kevin's work area, and ran back to the cottonwood grove.

I don't believe it was her intention to hide anything from me; it was her intention to fix it. She would fix it, she was thinking, because this was fixable, and it would be okay after she fixed it, and it would just be this big ol' story: *This one time, my sister fell inside a tree! How insanely weird is that? And I was all, say what? OMG! And I ran all the way to the garage and got a flashlight and climbed up there again, and I pulled her out, and she was okay, and we were all like OMG, like . . . that happened . . .*

"Annabel? Anna, I'm back! Hang on! It's okay. I'm coming."

Abbie scaled the tree and held her breath as she scrambled across the bridge. She clicked the headlamp on and held it over the abyss. The shadows gave way to deeper shadows. The whorled innards of the tree seemed to disappear into nothingness.

"Anna? *Annabel!*" Abbie kept calling, her heart pounding in her throat now. The cavity echoed back at her like a dry well. "Anna, please . . . please, answer me."

When there was no answer, Abbie swallowed hard and dropped the headlamp into the abyss, terrified of what she would see but needing to know. She watched it fall, down and down and down, clattering against the rotted wood, offering a few frightening glimpses of the endless chute far below, getting smaller and smaller, like a train disappearing down a long train track, until it struck something solid and flickered out. Abbie stared into the emptiness, stunned disbelief blossoming to panic.

"No ... how can that ... *No, no, no ... Annabel!*"

"Abbie?" Adelynn was getting scared. "What happened? Is Anna okay?"

"She fell. She fell down in there. *She's in there.*"

Cold horror. Consequences. It was all crashing down on Abbie. But now she knew what she had to do.

"Annabel, hold on," she called down into the dark. "Hold on, Anna. I will be right back. Do you hear me? I'm going to get Mommy. I'm coming right back, Anna, and I won't leave you."

Abbie clawed across the wide bridge and swung down through the branches again, but this time she missed the last one and dropped several feet to the uneven ground. Pain knifed upward from a hard twist of her ankle, but Abbie was already running, screaming, "Mommy! Mommy, come quick!"

Something talky was on the television in the bedroom. I had my back to it but was half listening to the background chatter while I sorted and folded the mountain of clean laundry into neat stacks on the bed. I had my system set up: Kevin's jeans and shirts, my jeans and shirts, Abbie's jeans and shirts, Anna's jeans and shirts, Adelynn's jeans and shirts, girl socks, mom socks, dad socks, pjs, bedding, bath towels, dish towels. I'd been moving it along like a machine since early afternoon, and I was almost done.

Supper was the next box on the flowchart, so that was probably on my mind. I don't specifically remember, but it was that time of day. Kevin would be home in ninety minutes or so. The girls had been outside for about an hour, but there was no need to call them in if they were having fun. The sun was setting, so they'd drift in soon enough.

I didn't hear Abbie screaming as she bolted over the grid and up the driveway, but to be totally honest, I wouldn't have flipped out even if I had. As the mother of three farm-raised tomboys, one of whom was afflicted with a chronic, life-threatening health issue, it's only prudent for me to ration my panic. When I hear someone screaming, it could mean anything from a dislocated finger to "the dog licked my pizza crust." I've learned to assess the situation calmly before I click into crisis mode.

"Mommy!" Abbie burst through the door. "Mommy, you gotta ... gotta come with me—right now. You gotta come outside."

"Just a sec," I said absently. "Let me finish this, and I'll be right out."

"No, Mommy, *now*. Anna's stuck in the tree. She's in the tree."

Something in her voice made me look up. Abbie gripped

her side, breathing hard from running, her face streaked with dirt and sweat. A flutter of unease went through my chest. Abbie was frantic, but what she was saying—*stuck in the tree*—I was thinking *stuck in a tree*, like you would assume a kid or a kitten or a kite would be *stuck in a tree*.

"Abbie, calm down," I said firmly. "Tell me what's wrong. Is she hurt? Is she bleeding?"

"No! I mean ... I ... I don't know. She's *trapped*."

"Well, I can't climb up there. She just needs help working her way down. Can you help her figure it out?"

"Mommy, you don't understand!" Abbie seized my arm. "You have to come out right now. *Come on.*"

"All right, calm down, sister. I mean it. Let me get my shoes on."

"No! Now! You have to hurry!"

With Abbie dragging at my arm, I managed to step into shoes on my way out the door. I was still operating on the assumption that Anna had climbed a little too high and was unable—or maybe just unwilling—to climb down. The sun dipped into the haze on the meadow as we hustled across the yard toward the cottonwood grove where Cypress barked and danced in nervous circles. I scanned the high branches, calling, "Annabel? Annabel, where are you? Abbie, I don't see her. Where is she?"

At the base of the tall cottonwood, Adelynn was on her hands and knees. She'd found a piece of metal pipe and was gouging desperately at the ground, clawing the loose dirt with her little hands.

"I'm digging her out, Mommy! I'm digging her out!"

It would have made more sense if she'd told me she was digging a hole to China. I swallowed hard and kept my voice as calm as possible.

"Girls . . . where is Annabel?"

"*There!*" In sheer frustration, they shrieked at me with one voice, stabbing grimy fingers toward the bottom of the trunk. "She is *in—the—tree!*"

Abbie still had a tight grip on my arm. She pulled me to the far side of the cottonwood and pointed to the gaping mouth thirty feet up.

"*There!*" She was beside herself now, pleading with me. "Mommy, do you see? She fell in there and went to the bottom."

It was incomprehensible. I didn't want to comprehend it. No part of me—not my brain, not my heart, not the laundry-folding Robo Mommy—no part of me wanted to accept this. But I recognized that pleading in Abbie's voice, that aching frustration, that pound-your-head-against-the-wall infuriating feeling of trying to make someone accept that all their assumptions are wrong, that the least dependable thing in the world is everything you thought you knew five minutes ago.

During our long journey to get a solid diagnosis for Anna, doctors told me again and again, "When you hear hoofbeats, you think horses, not zebras." Which is really just a catchall excuse for lazy, inside-the-box thinking. I grew to hate that old saying with a passion, but that moment in the cottonwood grove, I was thinking exactly the same way.

Maybe it's because we see these choices—consciously or

subconsciously—and it's human nature to choose the one that's less frightening.

Choice A: This giant tree, which I had assumed was a solid object, is actually a giant throat that just swallowed my child.

Choice B: Someone is playing a horrible prank on me.

My brain simply refused to let go of choice B.

When Anna first presented with acute symptoms of pseudo-obstruction motility disorder—a terrible distention of her belly along with intense pain—we made numerous trips to the pediatrician and then a gastroenterology specialist, and they always sent her on her way with the basic checkup and go-away over-the-counter symptom treatments. Ordinary tummy trouble stuff. But I had begun to understand that this was no ordinary tummy trouble. I wasn't willing to accept that label and watch her suffer. I kept pushing for a real diagnosis, so when no obvious diagnosis readily presented itself, the real trouble, they decided, was me. Given the choice between (1) mothers can be kinda crazy or (2) doctors don't know everything, many doctors in my experience go for option 1.

After one particularly grueling round of tests, a gastroenterologist happily summed up the non-results with a broad, "Good news, Mom! Everything's fine."

Six-year-old Anna huddled on my lap, exhausted and in pain. I stared blankly at the doctor's smiling face and echoed, "Everything's . . . *fine?*"

"That's good news, Mom." His smile faded to a stern scold. "That's something to be happy about."

"Look at her," I said. "She is not fine. *Please*. You have to help her."

"I've palpated her and felt no sign of obstruction. We've done bloodwork, upper and lower GI testing—look, sometimes moms just worry too much. They get nervous and ..." He studied me for a moment, then said carefully, "Sometimes, a mother can have a disorder called Munchausen's ..."

For a moment, it seemed like he was about to go on and explain to me what that means, but I'm pretty sure he could tell from the expression on my face that I knew darn well that *Munchausen by proxy* meant I was somehow making my child sick to gratify my own need for attention. He wisely backed down off that horse trailer. At the time, I was stricken with frustration—rage, to be honest—that he would even imagine I could hurt my child that way. I lay in bed that night, praying for a way to forgive, a way to move on and continue the fight for Anna's well-being. She was in misery, weak and vomiting. I made repeated calls to the doctor's surgery, telling them, "She's getting worse." They kept telling me the bowel prep for those tests always makes children feel sick. *She's fine*, they kept telling me, *she's fine, she's fine, she's fine. That bowel prep, yeah, that sure can make a kid sick, but she's fine.*

Late that night, Kevin and I mobilized care for Adelynn and Abbie (our great friends Nina and Paul Cash, who met us in the front yard like tag-team wrestlers), and we rushed Annabel to the hospital. Triage theories boiled down to the usual: "Think horses, not zebras."

Long story short, I lost it. I finally found inside me that roar God gave the mama bear. I don't know quite what I said, but I said it plain and in his face, and I made the point that a normal test result doesn't equal a healthy child, and a doctor not understanding something is not the same as that thing not existing.

"Fine," the ER doc huffed. "We'll do a few tests. If that's what it takes to make you happy, *Mom*."

The dismissive way they call me "Mom" always makes me wish their real mom would walk in and smack them round the head. No, I was not happy, but, yes, this was a step in the right direction. Even if the test showed something bad, knowing is better than not knowing. Knowing means you can do something about it.

I held Anna in my arms before and after X-rays and then a sonogram to confirm the results, and then we waited until they called Kevin and me into the little room where they take you when they have to tell you what you don't want to hear.

"I'm sorry," the ER doctor told us. "The intestine is 100 percent obstructed. The surgeon is on his way. You should prepare to be here for a long while."

Kevin and I were left standing there with the very real possibility that Anna would die that night.

Standing in the cottonwood grove four years later, I felt the same ringing in my ears as my head wrapped around the reality—the gravity—of what was happening.

The tree towered in front of me. Anna was somewhere inside it, close enough for me to reach out and touch her and still be utterly unreachable.

Abbie broke away from me, and before I could call her back, she was clambering back up the tree, agile as a squirrel. I sucked in a deep breath. Suddenly that branch seemed so much higher than I remembered. And the gaping grotto so much darker.

Chapter Four

Deep in the heart of the tree, Anna drifted, vaguely aware of the suffocating stillness and then . . . something else. Someone else. Somewhere else.

"I always thought Heaven would be like sitting on clouds," she told me later, "but it's like . . . it's like being suspended above the universe."

She was very circumspect and said very little about the experience. This wasn't like one of her long, spun-out recaps of a funny dream or a movie she'd seen. She confided only a few details on only a few occasions, and when she told me about it, I felt her weighing her words in a way that was very Annabel. This was the girl who used to look at the "Your Pain on a Scale of 1 to 10" chart and select the stoically moderate 6, even when all clinical indicators told us she was actually experiencing something more like a 9. She'd been through enough real drama in her short life; she had no interest in melodrama.

"Mommy, the gates of Heaven really are made of gold, and they really are big and bright."

When she confided in me and Kevin and Gran Jan in the days that followed—and in the years since then—she chose carefully what she wanted to share and what she wanted to keep to herself. And I respect that. I have never pumped her for details. I am curious—of course, I want to know the details as much as you do—but as the song says, "I can only imagine."

I imagine the pitch darkness dissolving to light around her, the dank air suffusing with pure oxygen, that prison cell of Earth and rotted wood giving way to clear blue sky, pure freedom. I close my eyes, and I can see her getting up from the muck, stepping into the City of God.

"I have always thought God has a big heart because He has so much love, and He does," she told me. "Mommy, He has a big heart that glows. God's heart was so filled with joy that it shined with ... with *gold glory*. And His eyes were like the biggest and most beautiful star in the sky."

The first of the evening stars were visible in the eastern sky as I ran across the open field, stumbled, caught myself, kept running, over the cattle grid to the gravel drive. I felt calm but fiercely focused on what needed to happen.

Find my cell phone.

Call Kevin.

Call 911.

Get Anna. Get my eyes on her. Get my arms around her.

I burst through the kitchen door, ran to my room, and

thrashed through the neat piles of laundry looking for my phone. My hands were trembling as I clicked to Favorites and speed-dialed Kevin's number. In the forever-long seconds it took him to answer, I was already out the door again, running down the driveway.

I called the veterinary clinic at 5:25 p.m., trying not to sound panicked when the receptionist answered.

"It's Christy. I need Kevin right away, please."

"He's right here. Hang on."

Knowing what I know now, this is another moment that sends a shiver down my spine. Kevin was supposed to be in surgery, performing a delicate operation on a large dog, but as the procedure got under way, he was concerned about the way the dog was responding to the anesthesia, and he stopped. This was a complex orthopedic surgery, and there was no one there who could have stepped in, so there's no way he would have scrubbed out once the procedure began. But the way things went, he happened to be standing right there at the front desk in his scrubs, talking to the dog's owner when I called.

"Hey, babe." Kevin's voice was like cool water.

"Kevin, Anna's in trouble."

I blurted out everything I knew about the situation—that she'd fallen into a hole in a tall tree, that I couldn't get to her—and even in the moment I think we were both surprised at how calm I sounded. Kevin immediately knew the tree I was talking about.

"I knew Abbie had been climbing up there, but I'm surprised Anna—"

49

"Please, just get here as quickly as you can. I'm calling 911."

"Hang on, hang on. I'll be there in ten," he said. "In less time than it would take them to get over here, I'll have a ladder up there and get her out."

I bit my lip, wanting to believe it would be that easy. "Please, hurry."

Kevin told me later that he envisioned climbing up a few branches, calming Abbie, reaching four or five feet into a depression and helping Anna down from the tree, no blood, no problem, just another Beam sisters misadventure that went over the line.

He could be right, I thought. We were assuming different answers to the same questions: Was she hurt? How deep did the chasm go? Abbie insisted that Anna had fallen all the way to the ground, but that didn't seem possible. How could a tree that large still be standing if the trunk was nothing but a hollow pipe? And if it was hollow but still solid enough to stand, could there be air inside? Regardless of how deep it was, the rotted core of a tree must be crawling with all kinds of creepy God-knows-what . . .

"Kevin, please, please hurry."

I knew he was only a few minutes away, but those few minutes were agony. Adelynn was alternately clinging to my leg and gashing at the ground with anything she could find. Abbie was sobbing, refusing to come down from her high perch. She kept crying out into the black hole—"Anna! Anna!"—begging Annabel to answer her.

Why didn't she answer?

"Having some trouble?" Our neighbor came through the trees, peering at Abbie in the twilit branches and me pacing below.

"Yes!" I ran to him, grateful to see another grown-up, even though we'd only met a few times in passing. Living in the country, there's a lot of space between people, but when someone needs help, the gap closes.

"Need a ladder?" he asked.

"Oh, yes, Jack, thank you. Please, hurry."

He was back in less than a minute, but when we propped the ladder against the tree, it was a good ten or twelve feet short of the branch where Abbie had posted herself like a sentry.

"Mommy," Abbie called to me. "I think she's—I don't think she can breathe."

I called Kevin again. "Kevin, I'm really getting scared. Abbie is at the top of the tree freaking out. She says Anna is having a hard time breathing. I can't stand here. I have to call 911. I have to do something."

"I'm here. I'm at the turnoff. Just sit tight and let me see what's going on."

The headlights on the borrowed diesel jalopy bounced across the pasture, closing the distance between us with a comforting roar. Kevin pulled to a stop and leaped out, leaving the bright lights directed toward the tree. On his way out of the animal hospital, he'd had the presence of mind to grab a great big rope they use to restrain horses for surgical procedures, but when he took in the situation—the true height of the tree, the inadequacy of even the tall ladder propped against it—he felt a jolt of nervous adrenaline. This might not be as simple as he thought.

Sprinting the quarter mile through the trees and over the field to his workshop, he was praying, willing himself to stay calm for his girls. Moments later, he came back to us on a dead run, panting hard, lugging a twenty-four-foot extension ladder on his shoulders.

"Abbie," he called, "c'mon down here now. You're not safe up there."

"I don't care!"

"Abigail. Get down here. Now."

"Daddy," she said wretchedly, "I'm scared. And I hurt my ankle. And I can't leave Anna, Daddy. I promised I wouldn't leave her."

"Okay." He rubbed one hand over his face, sweating despite the cool of the evening. "Hang on. I'm coming up there."

We positioned the ladder, extending it as high as it would reach, and Jack and I held it steady while Kevin scrambled up. I heard him talking to Abbie in his low, calm daddy voice, and after a moment, she let him help her down. It was dark now, and Abbie's bare legs were visibly shaking. When her feet were finally on the ground, I allowed myself to exhale.

"Kevin, did you see Anna? Is she breathing? Could you hear her?"

He shook his head grimly, striding toward the veterinary truck. I had to run to keep up with him.

"Kevin, I should call 911. Should I call?"

"I'll get her," he said. "Let's just stay calm."

He hitched a high-powered flashlight to his pocket, looped the rope over his shoulder, and headed back to the tree. With the twenty-four-foot ladder fully extended, Kevin was able to climb up and peek over the edge of the opening if he balanced on his toes on the very top rung—a sight in itself that stopped my heart.

Oh, God, please. Keep your hand on him. Keep him steady . . .

Running his hand along the jagged edges of rotting wood, Kevin still expected to find Anna relatively close to the hole. He was thinking that once he was at eye level, he'd be able to see her, and she'd be able to take the rope.

"Anna? Anna, Daddy's here. Everything's okay."

He looked up into the hollow of the tree above the hole, which gave him a sense of what the inside of the tree was like, but to look down, he'd have to climb higher. Kevin reached out with one arm and tested the branch where Abbie had been standing. When he shifted his weight to it, the branch moaned softly, and I covered my face with my hands.

"Oh, God! Please, be careful, Kevin!"

"Sit tight," he called to me, leaning into the cavity. "Everything's under . . . control . . ."

I heard his confidence leave him.

As Kevin beamed the flashlight down into the chasm, he saw what Abbie had seen. He'd grown up outdoors, climbed his share of trees, but he'd never seen anything like this. It was like staring down a dry well. Kevin's stomach dropped as his brain processed the truly dire straits Anna was in. He leaned in, but the corridor angled away from the light. There seemed to be no end to it.

"Anna? Can you hear me?"

He paused, straining to hear something. Anything. The only sound was the light wind in the leaves overhead.

"Okay, Anna." Kevin kept talking in that strong, soothing voice. "Okay, we got this. Daddy's here. Everything's going to be okay, baby."

I don't know if he was trying to convince her or himself or Abbie and Adelynn and me as we huddled shivering on the ground below.

Abandoning the ladder altogether, Kevin hoisted himself onto the wide branch and leaned most of his upper body into the hole. Trying not to dislodge chunks of the brittle rim, he stretched tentatively into the hole, like he was leaning into the mouth of a monster. He angled and tilted the light until he caught a glimpse of pink.

"*Jesus* ..." Kevin took in a strangled breath. "*Jesus, help me.*"

Anna was curled motionless in the dirt, in a fetal position, entombed in the bottom of the narrow wooden corridor. She looked lifeless and impossibly far away and very, very small.

Kevin dropped that great big rope that he'd thought was surely adequate for anything that could possibly be going on over here. I watched it spiral down to the scrub grass, as useless as a garden hose in a forest fire.

"Kevin? What's happening?"

"Christy. Call 911."

His voice was calm, but I know this man. I couldn't see his face, but I could feel his gut-deep fear.

"Nine-one-one, what is your emergency?"

The answer rushed out of me. Calmly. Firmly. Emergency room mother. No panic, but no wasted words.

"Stay on the line with me, okay, ma'am? I'm dispatching the volunteer fire department now. I want you to stay on the line with me until the first responders arrive."

"All right." I nodded at no one. "Yes. Okay."

I stood there, rooted to the spot, my phone frozen to the side of my face. In the background, I heard the dispatch radios and phones spreading the alarm. The operator came back, relaying questions from the paramedics, and I recited Anna's age, height, weight, blood type.

"Does your daughter have any existing medical problems?"

I made a soft, choked sound that was neither a laugh nor a cry. Or maybe it was a bit of both. "Yes. Yes, she does ..."

One gets the hang of explaining things after a while, but that first year, it was like trying to lay out the meandering plot of a soap opera. First came months of misery without any meaningful diagnosis or treatment. Then came a year with the gastroenterologist who saw Anna more times than I can count. He doggedly stuck with the "this mom tends to overreact" theory until the abdominal obstruction occurred. Even then, the pediatric surgeon we met in the emergency room had to practically twist his arm.

"But you just saw her yesterday and examined her and

sent her home. Now I've got her, and she is 100 percent obstructed. I'm seeing it on the X-ray, confirmed on the sonogram. It's confirmed. She's in serious trouble."

Kevin and I sat in ashen silence, listening to the ER doc on the phone in the hallway.

"Look, what the little girl always does or the mom always says—that's irrelevant. This is now, and she needs this surgery right now or she's not going to make it. Please. Help us help her."

His voice fell to an agitated murmur. It seemed like some tense words were being exchanged.

"What does all this mean?" I whispered to Kevin.

"She has a blockage of some sort in her intestines," he said. "They have to go in and release it surgically."

I didn't really understand what that meant yet—how seriously life-threatening this was—but I knew this was major, major surgery. Kevin's face had turned to a stern mask. I could tell he needed to think for a minute. *Anna* needed him to think. It was generally accepted that I was Chief of Little Girl Maintenance in our family, but Kevin spoke the language of diagnostics and biology. I depended on him to translate for me sometimes. But speaking the language of scalpels and surgery could be a blessing and a curse. Ignorance can be bliss, truth can be brutal, and helplessness is simply foreign to Kevin's nature. He sat there contemplating, elbows on his knees, fingers tented in front of his face, until the pediatric surgeon came back into the room.

We were presented with choosing between waiting for the

highly regarded specialist who knew Anna's history or placing our trust in this ER doctor we'd known for all of forty-five minutes.

Without hesitating, Kevin said, "Do the surgery."

It terrified me, but behind that terror, there was a weird sense of relief. We knew now what we were up against. We'd named the dragon, and we knew how to slay it. We could do the homework, make the decisions, and see her through this. Once she got through this operation, she'd be fine. Kevin even says, "I'm a surgeon at heart. A chance to cut is a chance to cure." That definitive, black-and-white solution was so appealing to both of us at that moment. In the years that followed, we'd have given anything for such cut-and-dried options.

I stroked Anna's forehead as controlled chaos—the tightly choreographed ballet of a surgical team—was set in motion all around us.

"We need to intubate her and suction the stomach before anesthesia." Someone in scrubs wedged between me and Anna's bed. "Dad, can you help us hold her?"

Kevin nodded and positioned himself with a firmly grounded grip on Anna, who was suddenly hyperaware and terrified. Thrashing and whimpering like a wounded animal, she fought with her last inch of free will as this big strange man she'd never seen before methodically forced a thick plastic tube up into her nose and down her throat.

"Swallow, Anna, *swallow*. We need you to swallow now," he kept barking like a drill sergeant. Meanwhile, Anna gagged and retched and vomited, struggling against Kevin, who held her in an unyielding grip, his face etched with sorrow.

I paced between the bed and the door, just trying to keep it together, digging my nails into my arms, biting my lip bloody to keep from yelling, *Stop it! Stop it! Get off her! You're hurting her!* They were helping her, I told myself numbly. Wasn't this what we'd been praying for? An answer? A resolution? *But why?* I begged God for understanding. *Why does it have to come at this terrible cost?*

"Anna, everything's going to be okay. I got you, Anna. Daddy's here."

Kevin's voice filled the room, low, sweet, and sonorous, filled with love and a specific brand of agony. Slow tears rolled down his face and dropped one by one into the tears that streamed from the corners of Anna's eyes.

Annabel's kind and gentle personality definitely comes from her daddy. "He's a middle child, like me," she likes to point out. He is a modern-day James Herriot who cares for all God's creatures, great and small. It was a bitter irony in his life, having a career as a healer and still being utterly unable to fix this tiny creature who was and is most dear to him.

God made mankind in his own image, we're told in Genesis. There have been many moments in my life when I saw that fleeting reflection. At this particular moment, I saw a father, heartbroken at what has to happen to his precious child, hearing her pleas—not ignoring them, never, never turning away—but knowing that this moment of anguish was part of a bigger plan.

Of all the names we have for God, maybe the most appropriate for those moments is the Aramaic word *Abba*, which most closely translates to "Daddy." *Abba* is the God we cry out to when we are at our smallest, our most vulnerable. *Abba* is the God whose heart we break, the God who weeps for us and says, "Daddy's here."

"It's okay, baby. Anna, Daddy is here for you. Everything's going to be okay."

It was dark now in the cottonwood grove. The headlights from the truck cast a watery haze of yellow illuminating the ground around us. Kevin held the flashlight inside the broken grotto at the top, making the tree into a tall, dim candle in the dark woods. It was just enough light to show me his face as he leaned in, talking and talking to Anna in that sweet and sonorous *Abba* way.

Over the past four years, they'd developed a unique bond, daddy to daughter, during some intensely difficult times. They spent many dark nights, not always speaking but always communicating, knowing what needed to be done—the quick repair of an IV, an adjustment to the naso-gastric tube—knowing that sometimes it hurts. Anyone who's had to care for a chronically ill child knows what I'm talking about. Anna understood. Kevin came to be grateful for her courageous, unshakable spirit, but it left a scar on his soul.

"Anna, look at me. Can you look at Daddy? C'mon. Show me that you can hear me, Anna. Can you move your arm? Show me you can move your arm, baby."

Waiting the agonizing half hour for the response teams to

find their way to us in the maze of dark country roads, Kevin was forcing himself to be a doctor. Assess her condition. Determine if she was . . .

No. Neither of us was willing to allow that possibility.

Far below, in the sliver of light, he could see Anna lying there. She looked peaceful. There was no obvious misalignment of her arms and legs, no significant blood loss that he could see. Everything in his gut was telling him that she was alive, but his medical mind was doing the sums, factoring in how far she'd fallen, calculating the vanishing odds of anyone coming away from that without head trauma, internal bleeding, some kind of devastating spinal cord injury. He wasn't ready to process the less immediate psychological impact of being effectively buried alive.

"*Annabel!*" He called her name, and there was a hint of drill sergeant in it now, a tone of authority our girls know better than to ignore. "Anna, do as I tell you. Move your arm, Anna. Move your arm. Show me you can hear me. Right now, Anna, *you show me.*"

She didn't look up, didn't flinch or shift her position, but her arm moved. She raised one limp hand up from the dirt and set it down. Kevin whooped out loud, praising God for that small miracle.

"Christy! She's alive. She moved her arm."

"Oh, God," I breathed. "Thank you, God."

Kevin stayed there, watching from his perch high in the jagged grotto, scanning the rolling darkness for the distant lights of the ambulance and fire crew. She didn't call out to him, but he knew she was alive. That was all he needed. He felt Anna's serenity, the way he did during all that wordless *togetherness* they had shared through so many dark hours. He allowed her quiet spirit to calm his pounding heart.

Sirens wailed, coming closer, and soon heavy tires sprayed gravel on the turnoff to the driveway.

"Anna, I have to get down now," Kevin told her quietly, "but I'll be right here. Mommy and I are right here, baby, just a few feet away, and we're praying for you, and we're waiting for you. It'll be okay soon."

Annabel lay still, never moving, not responding.

Chapter Five

I love the story about the day when Jesus, who could have been doing other things that other people deemed bigger and more important, chose to spend his time with a group of little children. Some guys started raising a stink about it, and Jesus said, *Let the little children come to me, for such is the kingdom of God. Truly I tell you, anyone who will not receive the kingdom of God like a little child will never enter it* (Luke 18:16–17).

The Bible says very little about people entering or even seeing Heaven and living to tell about it: Ezekiel and Isaiah had prophetic visions and were overwhelmed by the glory of God. John says he saw the Holy City in Revelation. Paul tells about a friend who was "caught up into Paradise and heard inexpressible words." Stephen said he saw Heaven, and he was promptly dragged out and stoned to death. Clearly, it's a sensitive topic—maybe because people in our cynical world have such a hard time receiving it like little children.

"The way I saw Heaven was ..." Anna thought hard, searching for words when she told me months later. "It's hard to describe. But Jesus really does have a brown beard and an old-time white cloth robe that ... I think it is a little ripped at the bottom, but I can't remember exactly because that was all the way back during Christmas break."

You remember how that is. A thousand years are as a day when school is out.

Another thing Annabel once told me: "I want to play French horn. It has the same word as French fry!" She sees the world as only a child can, and she saw Heaven the same way. She received it exactly the way Jesus hoped we all would: on faith. I don't press her to talk about it, but I find myself pondering the expression of the inexpressible, the look of love on Jesus' face as He put His arms around her and brought her onto His lap.

From the time they were babies, my girls have been shown countless images of Jesus: iconic paintings, like the one that illustrates that story from Luke, and more modern takes that are probably a more accurate depiction of his skin tone. At Sunday school and church, they've been told the stories. They've seen the classic movies and watched documentaries on family-friendly cable channels.

But I'd like to think that when Annabel saw Jesus standing there, she knew Him with her heart. Because He already knew her heart so well.

Anna being Anna, she quickly cut to the chase and asked Jesus: "Can I see the creatures?"

"Creatures? What creatures?"

"You know," said Anna, "the ones with the body of a lion and the head of an eagle."

"*No.*" (Did He smile at that, I wonder?) "*No, you cannot see the creatures.*"

"Mommy, He told me no!" She stressed that point when she was telling me about this part, unpleasantly surprised, because in her mind, Heaven is where everything is yes, and now her very first request—a relatively simple one, to her way of thinking—had been turned down without much due process.

"*You have to go back, Anna. It's not your time.*"

"But I don't want to," Anna said. "I don't want to go back."

"*I know you don't want to go. But I have plans for you to complete on Earth that you can't complete if you're in Heaven . . .*"

He knew why she wanted to stay. He had to have known. Kevin and I never doubted that He heard us all those nights we spent crying out to Him when Anna was in agony. We started out with formal requests for healing; eventually we were broken down to begging for even an hour of relief. We just couldn't understand why, why, why He kept telling us no.

For Him to tell Anna no in this moment, face-to-face, after all she'd seen and heard in this place—to expect her to leave this place of gold glory for a place of pain and anguish—it must have been incomprehensible to her. It was certainly incomprehensible to us as we watched her suffer. *No* seems to be the one thing we have no trouble receiving like little children.

*

"I hear sirens," I told the emergency operator. "I think they're here."

"Okay, good. Just stay on the line with me, ma'am. Don't hang up until the first responders get there."

The first unit from the Briaroaks Volunteer Fire Department arrived a little after 6:30 p.m. Seeing Kevin's truck on the far side of the field, they made their way over to the cottonwood grove, steering around the stumps and gullies as well as they could without slowing down. Bryan Jamison, the burly Briaroaks chief, was right behind them.

I ran over to the unit and asked, "Are you the first responders?"

Okay, I know. Duh. But appreciate the moment I was in.

"Yes, ma'am," said one of the young men. "We got a call that someone had fallen."

"Yes! Please, hurry. She's over here." Before I clicked off the cell phone, I said to the operator, "Yes, it's them. They're here. The responders are here."

"Okay, good. It's gonna be okay, all right? Stay calm and"—she cleared her throat gruffly—"God bless you, ma'am."

I took that small prayer with me as I tramped back through the trees, followed by the two young men, who looked comfortingly capable—young, strong, and geared up—the kind of corn-fed Texans who could either climb this tree or tear it down if needed. They beamed flashlights on the ground, looking more and more confused as Kevin hustled down the ladder to meet them.

"We got a call," the first responders said again, but this

time it sounded like a question. "Something about a little girl in a tree?"

It took them a few minutes to wrap their heads around the situation—as it had for Kevin and me. I had tried to make the dispatcher understand, and she did communicate to them that it was more than a medical call, but this was the ultimate "think zebras" moment; the reality of it was a little lost in translation. Generally a call that someone has fallen takes first responders to a scene where an elderly person has fractured a hip or broken a wrist. Even being told "a little girl fell from a tree" brings something completely different to mind. The last thing they would assume is that the tree opened up and swallowed the little girl like a catfish swallows a minnow.

As the responders were absorbing this, the Briaroaks fire engine roared across the pasture. The crew, led by Lieutenant Mike Hill, launched into the same sort of controlled chaos that had surrounded the surgical team: a highly trained, no-nonsense ballet. There was barely a shred of light on the horizon now, so their first priority was lighting the area. They pulled as close as they could to the trees and left all the vehicle headlights blazing, but it was still shadowy and dim in the grove. Hefting large portable lights off the engine, they ran thick electrical cables from the truck. The immense cottonwood towered in the floodlights, ghostly pale wood showing through the chunky bark.

Rooted to the spot where I would spend most of the next two hours, I watched them hoist their ladder up next to Kevin's. They called up and down to each other, taking measurements, assessing Anna's condition—to the extent they could—weighing all the risks and probabilities. Questions had been crowding my brain as I waited. Most of them were asked and answered in the first ten minutes the responders were on the scene. We were all worried about the same dark possibilities.

Did she have enough oxygen? The fact that she'd responded to Kevin told us she had enough to stay alive, at least for the moment.

How badly was she hurt? Anna's silence frightened us more than the sound of her screaming would have. Kevin hadn't observed any significant blood loss or obviously misaligned bones, but from that distance with virtually no light on her, it was hard to tell. The inside of the tree wasn't straight and even; it was slanted and irregular with knots and protrusions that cast deep shadows, even if you managed to lean way in, maneuvering and twisting the flashlight just so.

What about head and spinal cord injury? Again, there was no way to tell and no way to observe proper spinal injury protocol while they extracted her. The harsh reality was that she'd fallen face-first, thirty feet to solid ground; the possibility of her walking away without serious injury was very slim. In light of that, Mike Hill, the engineer on the rescue, made the call: an ambulance would be standing by together with a helicopter ready to fly Anna to the hospital in Fort Worth.

Of course, there was the big question: How do we get her out?

The Briaroaks crew had two ladders, both of which were tall enough to reach the third floor of a building. When they were fully extended, the top rung on one ladder rested against the side of the bridge branch, and the top rung on the other rested against the crumbling lower lip of the open grotto. Standing below them, I could see the bits of bark and moss dropping down as Mike scaled the ladder and leaned into the hole.

"Anna? Annabel," he called. "I'm a fireman. My name is Mike. I came to get you. Can you hear me? Anna, can you answer me?"

Working the flashlight between the twisted shadows, Mike eventually caught a fleeting glimpse of pink. He worked himself a bit lower into the tree and focused the beam of his flashlight on Anna, sitting with her back to the inner wall of the tree, arms around her legs, her forehead resting on her knees.

"I see her! I got her," he called over his shoulder. "She's sitting up. Appears to be conscious. Anna? Annabel! Can you look up here? Hey, Anna, look up here and wave to me."

Calling Anna's name over and over again, he got no response.

"Annabel, my name's Mike. Do you hear me? I'm here, and your mom and dad are here, and we're all working on getting you out of there, okay? I'm not gonna leave you, Anna. We're gonna get you out, and it'll be okay. Just sit tight and don't be scared, okay? Anna? Annabel, look up here and—okay, she looked up! She looked up at me for a second."

Later Mike told us she had turned her face, a blank stare, up toward him for a moment or two before she lowered her face to her arms again, and she stayed that way without moving for most of the next two hours. He stayed, too, even though his legs were burning with fatigue and his back ached. From thirty feet away with the twisted shadows inside the tree, the flashlight couldn't have given her much relief from the pitch darkness, but he was unwilling to leave her without it.

There was a brief notion that someone might be lowered in to get her, but the thinnest person on the crew was a guy named Tristan Nugent, a muscled-up twelve-stone dude. There was no way he was fitting in there, even without his gear. The idea was quickly discarded, along with any thought of cutting into the tree with drills or chainsaws. Given our limited vision of what the tree was actually like inside, the risk of it partially or completely collapsing on her was too great.

They discussed various ways to lower something down for her to tie onto herself. Someone suggested a rope with some kind of slipknot or noose at the end, but Kevin didn't like the sound of that.

"She can't tighten it around her waist with the pain and distention in her belly," he said. "If she's too weak to hold on or if she passes out, it could get up around her neck."

"Do you think she'd be able to get herself into a harness of some kind?" Bryan asked, and Kevin nodded.

"I think so. If it's physically possible, she'll make it happen."

"Helicopter!" Adelynn pointed up at the sound of thrumming blades overhead.

A spotlight swept the pasture for a flat place to land. The twin-engine helicopter circled and swooped like a seagull, hovered briefly over a bald patch, and set down halfway between the gravel drive and the cottonwood grove. Dry leaves and dust rippled out from the whirring blades. It powered down to an idle, but they kept it running so they'd be ready to take off. That relentless noise was like a single driving heartbeat as the crew moved about the grove, securing the ladders, passing rope and radios, talking on cell phones.

In addition to the two first responders on the rescue truck, Bryan, the Briaroaks chief, plus the crew of three on the Briaroaks engine, there were two paramedics in the ambulance and a crew of three—the pilot, a flight nurse, and another paramedic—on board the helicopter. At some point someone put the other dogs in the house, but Cypress would not be moved. He paced well out of the way but never out of earshot, half sitting on his trembling haunches, pacing again, his eyes riveted on the tree.

Kevin and the fire crew set about fashioning the harness from a thick blue rope and rigging a pulley system they could use to lift Anna out. There was concern that too much movement up and down the ladders might put undue stress on the branch and contribute to the breakage on the lower lip of the opening, so Tristan and Mike, two crew members from the Briaroaks engine, climbed up and didn't come down.

"Anna, can you hear me? Anna, can you look up here for me?" Mike kept calling, and every once in a while he'd report, "Okay, she's responding. I did see a response there."

It was after 7:00 p.m. now. She'd been inside the tree for about two hours.

Seeing the royal blue of Kevin's surgical scrubs under the rigged lights, I realized that at some point, he'd put his coat around my shoulders. A hard, deep shiver went through me, and I closed my eyes for a moment. *Don't you do it, Lord. Don't you answer her prayer. Don't take her like this.*

"Mrs. Beam?"

I felt a touch on my elbow. It was one of the paramedics.

"I'm sorry, ma'am, I need you to come over to the ambulance with me," he said. "Your daughter needs you."

"My daughter . . ."

"Your older girl, ma'am. She seems to be having a panic attack."

My feet still felt rooted to the spot where I'd been standing since the rescuers arrived. It was all I could do to tear my eyes away from that hole in the tree, but I forced myself to follow him. The back of the ambulance was wide open, and I could see Abbie inside, lying on a trolley. Under the fluorescent lights, she looked ashen and small. As I approached, I could hear her sobbing hysterically through the oxygen mask that covered her face.

"We gave her some oxygen," said the paramedic, "but we can't seem to get her calmed down. We need you to either release her from our care or let us take her to the hospital."

"Oh, Abbie, sweetie ..." I clambered up into the back of the ambulance, asking over my shoulder, "Could I please talk to her in private for a minute?"

He nodded and stepped aside to swing the door shut. I scrunched down on the floor by the trolley so I could get my arms around her. Abbie was cold, shaking with sobs that wrenched the air in and out of her chest.

"Please, Abbie ... Abigail, *shhhhh* ... please, you have to relax. Just chill out, breathe in, breathe out. Abigail, breathe with me. Inhale ... exhale ... good girl. Keep breathing with me. In through the nose ... out through the mouth ..."

I stroked her back and rubbed her arms, crooning and hushing. It was probably all of three minutes, but I was aching to get back to Annabel, and I realized with shame and sorrow that this scant three minutes of comfort was more indulgence than Abbie had required of me in the past four years combined. She was eleven years old, but she thought and acted with the maturity and seriousness of a little adult.

"Abbie has an old soul," we always say when we're talking about her solid instincts, her natural generosity, her innate intelligence.

There was also this role in which she was cast: the big sister. Abbie rose to every occasion, every time an additional responsibility was prematurely foisted on her because we had to rush off to an emergency room or a doctor's appointment in Boston. We never wanted her and Adelynn to feel like the "other" sisters, and we went out of our way to devote time and attention to them whenever we could, trying our best to balance the way our lives had come to revolve around Anna's health issues. But since when was "whenever we could" enough for any kid?

In the days following that initial surgery on Anna's intestines, I was weary but hopeful. Kevin doesn't wear his heart on his sleeve, but he has a very healthy way of processing every-thing as needed; he contemplates all the possibilities, privately prays, weeps, curses—whatever he needs to do. I tended to stuff everything into an emotional storage locker, promising myself that I would deal with it later. This surgery would fix everything, I told myself. We just had to get through these next few weeks of recovery, and for that, I called on my inner Robo Mom.

The surgeon told us that at some point, Anna's appendix had "gotten sick," and I thought of several times I'd taken her to the doctor's or emergency room with pain, fever, and vomiting. On one or more of those occasions, the appendix must have been horrifically infected, leaking into her abdomen. As it healed itself, it had formed a thick cord of scar tissue that adhered to the small intestine and constricted as her body grew. After a time, there was only a small pas-sageway left, which explained why Anna did well with liquids but couldn't tolerate solid food, which made her stomach distend like a balloon.

The tipping point was the thick milk shake of bowel prep stuff she'd been forced to consume for the endoscopy. You remember—the one where "everything was *fine*" except for me and my fussy insistence that something was really, really wrong. The weight of that was more than her system could take and caused the complete obstruction.

Kevin listened quietly. I couldn't understand why he still seemed so stressed. I felt like I was breathing with both lungs for the first time in a year. All that frustration and anger and Internet research and begging to be heard—it had gradually formed a vise grip on the back on my neck, and in one cool rush of relief, I felt it let go. Everything the surgeon was saying made so much sense to me. I'd been so hungry for that clear explanation. A simple diagnosis. A plain path forward. Happily ever after.

"Our prayers have been answered!" I told Abbie and Adelynn on the phone.

I wasn't ready to hear that the answer was no.

Reality set in as the days in the hospital dragged on. I was eager for this nightmare to be over. I wanted us to get back to normal, and I had my fantasy definition of "normal" all figured out. Apparently, God did not get this memo.

Anna didn't get better. She got worse.

Once again, her little belly swelled, and she sank into a haze of sleepless pain, surviving on sips of liquid and IV fluids. She wanted to lie in bed and be left alone, but Kevin and I wheedled and nagged. We cajoled her to her feet several times a day and marched her around the fourth floor of the hospital in an attempt to kick-start her digestive system. A few days after the surgery, Annabel suffered a pruritic reaction—an all-over skin-crawling itchiness—from the morphine, which then had to be taken away from her, and the painkillers she could still tolerate gave her very little relief.

That Sunday, March 9, 2008, the pediatric surgeon came by to check on Annabel. When I saw him in a dapper three-piece suit instead of the customary surgical scrubs, I smiled and said, "Well, good morning! You're in your Sunday go-to-meetin' clothes."

"I was in church this morning, and I couldn't stop thinking about Annabel," he said. "I thought I'd stop by for a minute and . . ."

His smile faded as he laid a practiced hand on her forehead. He summoned a nurse, who checked Anna's vitals. Her temperature had spiked to 102.7°F. She was in great pain, distended and pale, and when the surgeon palpated her tummy, she flinched in agony.

"Pinging," he said to Kevin, moving a stethoscope over Anna's midsection.

"What does that mean?" I whispered.

"When there's extra gas and no healthy gut sounds," Kevin said, "sometimes you hear pinging."

"And that means?"

"Something's wrong."

Her intestines were fully obstructed again, and would require surgery to open up her abdomen once more. Within minutes, the whole surgical ballet repeated itself. The anesthesiologist came to talk us through the surgery, and I was relieved when he gave Annabel the first component of the cocktail that would step her down to unconsciousness. I leaned in close to nuzzle her ear, the way I used to nuzzle the precious little seashell ears of all my baby girls, whispering that heartfelt prayer of blessing from the book of Numbers.

"The Lord bless you and keep you. The Lord make His face to shine upon you and be gracious unto you. The Lord lift up His countenance upon you . . . and give you peace."

Kevin kissed her cheek and whispered, "Bye, baby. See you soon."

As they wheeled her bed from the room, he took my hand. Sorrow poured from my heart like water from a breached levee, and I cried for a long, bitter while. Gathered in the waiting room were precious family and friends, beautiful souls who love Kevin and me like siblings and love our girls like their own.

My brother Greg and his wife, Jill, had been caring for Abigail and Adelynn at their house in Wichita Falls and had brought them to the hospital to be handed over to Nina, one of several great friends who took turns caring for the girls so Kevin and I could camp out in Annabel's hospital room. Kevin's sister, Corrie, was holding Adelynn (three years old at that time) when Scott, our pastor from Alsbury Baptist Church, walked in. When Adelynn saw him, she flashed a sunbeam smile, reached out her arms, and said, "I want God to hold me!"

We all burst out laughing. It was such a perfect moment. We all knew exactly what Adelynn was thinking; we talked every week about going to "God's house," and when we got there, right up front was this guy who seemed to be hosting the party, shaking hands at the door as people arrived and departed. Adelynn received that like a child and drew the logical conclusion. Now she needed to be held by this big someone who made her feel safe and loved.

I think everyone in the room could relate. We'd all been through so much by this time, Adelynn's frank little demand cracked us up and broke the tension, but as the laughter made us breathe, her words resonated like a bone-deep prayer: *I want God to hold me.* We laughed till we cried, and then we cried until we laughed again.

After what seemed like a thousand hours, Kevin and I were taken to meet with the surgeon in the same room where we'd met him nine days earlier. I remember thinking how easily we become creatures of habit. We sat in the same chairs, staring at the familiar white-on-white wall-paper, feeling the layers of bad news that had been spoken and heard under the generic artwork and anatomical diagrams.

The surgeon came in looking exhausted and grim.

"When organs and abdominal tissue stick together, adhesions—bands of fibrous tissue—sometimes form. We found severe interlooping adhesions ... required extensive dissection to free ..." After that, the words came and went in waves like an outgoing tide. "... separated and placed the intestine back in the abdomen ... because there was no definitive cause for the second obstruction ... continue to have adhesions ... that she may not recover in a manner giving a strong quality of life."

"Wait—what?" I squeezed my eyes shut and opened them wide, trying to take it in. What he was saying. This thing he couldn't be telling me. "You're saying ... this will keep happening *for the rest of her life*? You're saying that from now on ... this *is* her life?"

"I'm saying we may have to continue to release the adhesions through surgery."

"But why is this happening?" I pressed him. "I don't understand what would cause something like this to happen."

"The gastroenterologist will be in to talk with you about it. If we're looking at a motility disorder, that can be very difficult to diagnose. The testing is invasive. You wouldn't want to put a kid through that unless you absolutely have to. Once it's diagnosed, it can be a lifelong battle."

Kevin asked the relevant clinical questions. The surgeon gave guarded clinical answers. I sat still, my mind reeling through the day-to-day realities beyond all that jargon. I saw the landscape of Annabel's life being razed before my eyes. The landscape of our own lives—Kevin's and mine. And Abigail's. And Adelynn's.

Our family had been torn apart. Abbie and Adelynn had been living out of their little backpacks for almost two weeks, chronic sleepover guests on a rotating schedule that now dropped off the edge of the calendar into an unknowable future. Kevin's partners at the veterinary clinic were amazingly supportive—never questioning that family comes first—but Kevin hated imposing on them week after week, month after month.

Year after year.

But all that shrank to a footnote; the shadow overwhelming everything was the suffering Annabel would have to endure. The invasive procedures. The scarring surgeries. The slow erosion of her goofy, shining spirit. It was wrong.

Like trying to breathe water or swim through solid rock. Impossible and broken and *wrong, wrong, wrong.*

Kevin and I kept it together pretty well while talking with the surgeon and then allowed ourselves to be ushered to the surgical waiting area where our friends and family sat talking in low murmurs, gentle laughter, soft prayers. The men immediately stood and went to Kevin, and the women took me in like a warm patchwork quilt. Oh, I wanted God to hold me, and He sent His best possible emissaries. I started to tell them what the surgeon had told us, but as the words came out, they became as real as cinder blocks, and they were too heavy for me. My sweet sisters let me gasp and stammer through it, and then they let me cry.

With so many tubes and wires in and out of her body, Annabel looked like a little pink butterfly in a spiderweb. A tube that traveled up her nose and down into her stomach provided suction for drainage. Rectal and urinary catheters performed the obvious functions. Two small tubes in her nostrils pushed oxygen into her lungs as pneumonia threatened. A PICC line (an IV catheter that goes directly to the heart) was inserted just below Annabel's collarbone to deliver nutrients she couldn't get any other way. Her body blossomed with deep purple bruises as one vein after another was blown. Nutrient-providing IV fluids are thicker than saline, and the veins can take that for only so long. Anna hadn't eaten for fifteen days. Feeding her with IV fluids wasn't going to cut it for the long haul.

That's where we were then. The long haul.

Abbie was eight years old then: too small to understand,

but big enough to do as she was asked—and we had to ask a lot of her. She became my right arm at home and Adelynn's second-string mommy when I wasn't around. She was also the spark of joy that kept us from getting morose, a little lighthouse who kept us oriented toward what childhood is supposed to be. She never saw or treated Anna like anything less than Anna. She prodded her sisters to play and giggle and be interested in having fun, and her endless imagination flew Anna away from unpleasant reality.

I recall one of the good days when Anna was feeling well enough to play and Abbie was able to nudge her outside for the afternoon. At suppertime, they came in, wonderfully sweaty and dirty, smelling of sunscreen and dry grass.

"Mommy," Annabel enthused, "Abbie and Adelynn and I played a game where we had to get to the top of this tree in order to save the world!"

"Abbie, breathe with me. In through the nose ... out through the mouth ..."

In the back of the ambulance, I gripped Abbie's hand, keeping my voice low and warm, hating the moment of tough love that I knew was coming, hating all the tough-love moments that had already come and gone.

"Abigail, we can't do this right now," I said firmly. "We need to keep it together now. You've got to get a hold of yourself. If you can't breathe, they'll have to take you to the hospital, Abbie, and I can't go with you."

"I don't want to go." Hiccuppy sobs caught in her throat. Abbie knotted her fists in her lap. "I *won't* go. I have to be here for Anna when she comes out. I have to be here for Adelynn when you all go to the hospital. But I'm scared, Mommy. I'm so scared ..."

"I know. I know, but—"

"You don't know," she choked through her tears. "You don't know."

"What don't I know? Tell me so I can understand."

"It's all my fault."

"No. It is not." I put my hands firmly on her shoulders and sat her up to face me. "Listen, sister. None of this—ever—has ever been your fault, not one bit of it. Why would you even think that?"

"Because I told her ... I told her to get in there." Abbie pulled the oxygen mask away from her face, and the whole story came out in a guilty, breathless rush. "It started to crack, and I told her ... I said I would get around her and go down the big tree, and then my weight would be off the branch, and she could cross over and go down the way she came up, and I thought it was only a little bit in there, like a foot or something, and I just needed her to step in there for a second so I could get around her, and she kept saying no, and I kept saying *just go*, and then she did, and she ... she ... she didn't want to do it, and I made her do it, Mommy. I made her get in, and it'll be my fault if she's—"

"Abbie, no. *Abbie*, listen to me. First of all, that was a great plan. That was a brilliant plan, and I love that you thought of it. Because you were looking out for her, like you always do. You had no way of knowing it was going to turn out like this. Abbie, sometimes, even if we try to do everything right—

82

even when we *do* do everything right—sometimes things still turn out all wrong. And all we can do then is regroup. You gotta regroup now, Abbie. You need to let go of everything you can't control. Anything that's already happened, anything you're afraid might or might not happen—you can't control any of that. You can only control how you react to it. And how you're reacting right now, Abbie—I can't fix it for you. Only you can fix it. And you can, Abbie. You are a strong person, physically and emotionally and mentally. You can fix this."

Abbie nodded, trying to swallow, trying to stay with me.

"Anna is going to be okay." I made her look me in the eyes, and I made myself believe what I was saying. "God's hand is on her. No matter what. You know that, right?"

"But what if . . . what if she's not okay?"

"That's why I have to stay, Abbie. You understand that, don't you?"

She nodded again and pushed the heel of her hand across her cheek; she was still bleak but breathing somewhat evenly. In through her nose. Out through her mouth. I kissed her temple and took her hands between mine and asked her, "Will you pray with me?"

Abbie nodded. I touched my forehead to hers.

"Heavenly Father . . . please . . . we need your peace. And your strength. And your love. Please let your peace come over Abbie. Calm her heart, Lord, and her soul . . . and help her breathe. And help me . . . help me be . . . whatever I need to be now. And be with Anna. Please, keep her in your care and let her know she's not alone."

We sat still for a long moment. There was no sound but

the thrumming heartbeat of the helicopter outside. After a while, Abbie put her arms around my neck, and I hugged her tight, willing her to know how I cherished her, not willing to be the first one to let go.

When she pulled away, I said, "Okay?"

Abbie said, "Okay."

And I knew she would be. But I also knew now that her life hung in the balance, too, her fate tied to Anna's in a way that none of us could truly understand. As we climbed out of the back of the ambulance, I silently said another prayer for both of them.

"Annabel."

"Yes?"

She's smart, my Annabel. I suspect she knew there was a moment of tough love coming.

"Anna, it is time for you to go back."

"I don't want to go. I want to stay with you."

"It's time for you to go, Annabel. The firemen are going to get you out, and when they do . . . Anna, you will be totally fine. There will be nothing wrong with you. My Holy Spirit will be with you. Don't be afraid. I'm sending my guardian angel to be with you."

Annabel received His promise like a child. On faith.

"Anna? Annabel . . ."

A faraway voice was calling her name.

"I'm a fireman. I came to get you. Can you hear me? Anna, can you answer me?"

She opened her eyes. The gold glory was gone. Annabel was alone in the darkness.

Chapter Six

In the belly of the tree, Anna scrambled to her feet, trying to breathe, but the air was closed up and earthy. A tiny dot of light pierced the darkness above her, she told me later, and she thought it might be an open knot in the tree and that if she could reach it, she might be able to put her mouth to it and take a breath. A narrow ledge jutted about eight inches from the wall just above her head.

"Like if I were right here," she said, outlining a spot on the rug, "there would be this ledge inside the tree, like here." She held her hand flat just above her forehead. "And I tried to get up on it, because I thought if I could get up there, maybe I could find a way out. But it was really small and hard to get up there. Slippery. Because everything was all muddy."

It was observed in the ER later that her nails were embedded with moss and dirt from her clawing effort to climb onto that ledge.

"I bet that was scary," the nurse said, but Anna just smiled.

"It was dark," she told me the next day, "but Jesus sent an angel. So once I came back, I could see inside the tree."

Once I came back, she said, as matter-of-factly as she would refer to hopping off the school bus at our gravel drive.

The angel wasn't what Anna expected an angel to be.

"She looked more like ... like a fairy, I guess. And then she got more and more clear, and then it was like—Mommy, God *winked* at me through the body of the angel. And I knew He was saying to me, *I'm going to leave you now and everything's going to be okay*. And then the angel got, like, solid again, and she stayed with me the whole rest of the time. She shined a light so I could see the inside of the tree where I was. I could see the walls then, and they were like this ..."

Here Anna made a motion with her hands, showing me the tree's mysterious inner world, which I eventually saw for myself after Kevin climbed up there on a sunny day with a light and a camera. The inside of the tree is actually quite beautiful; the soaring walls are marbled and muscled, flowing with shades of ebony and mahogany and ghostly white.

"The feel of it was hard and smooth but scratchy in parts," said Anna. "Like soft, but then hard. Like firewood that's been split. And the floor was just kind of muddy."

On the ground, half hidden by mud and roots, was the headlamp Abbie had dropped down to her two hours earlier. Annabel sat down and fiddled with it for a while but couldn't figure out how to make it work. And that was okay, she said.

She didn't need it. They just sat quietly together, Anna and her angel, surrounded by a halo of silent light.

"And that's how I was able to grab the rope," Anna said. "The only way I could get a hold of it was because my guardian angel shined her light on it."

I'd resumed my post below the grotto. Kevin remained on the move, checking in with members of the team, coming by every once in a while to grip my hand. Abbie stood nearby, one protective arm around Adelynn's shoulders. Two of the rescue workers still on the ground had given Abbie and Adelynn their coats, a small gesture that meant a lot as the night air cooled enough for us to see our breath when we prayed.

The plan for getting Anna out safely—an engineering feat that involved ropes, ladders, pulleys, and a lot of patient expertise—evolved as a coordinated effort between crew members on the ground and on the ladders with Kevin somewhere in the middle of it all. Problems were analyzed and solved as they arose.

First, they came up with a little harness they hoped she'd be able to tie herself into. It was like the seat of a baby swing, essentially, fashioned from thick but pliable rope that would hold her weight but wouldn't get snagged on the jagged ridges and outcroppings inside the tree. Then the crumbling lower lip of the opening had to be taken into consideration. If it broke away, the shards would rain down on Anna's head. If it cut into the rope as they hauled her up, it could fray and break when she was high enough to be even more seriously injured than she already was. Not knowing the extent of her injuries, they had to be painstakingly slow as they brought her up; it was imperative that there be no jolting movements to her neck and spine, no quick upward lurches that might crack her head on the irregular walls.

"The real problem is when we get her up to the top," I heard someone telling Kevin. "We can't just drag her over the ledge. We need to establish a second point of contact so we can take her all the way up and then swing her out."

They would need a taller ladder, they realized, along with another pulley.

It's funny how God sometimes hears our prayers before we even know what we're supposed to pray for. As the Briaroaks crew prepared to drop the harness down to Anna, a call came in from the dispatcher. Another agency had dispatched the Cleburne Fire Department by mistake about twenty minutes earlier. The Cleburne engine was halfway to our place now, and they were on the radio, asking if they should turn around and go back or continue on over, just in case we needed a few extra hands. They had a forty-five-foot ladder and pulley system on board.

Bryan relayed the news up the ladder to Mike and Tristan and told the dispatcher, "Tell them to come on over. We're ready to start bringing her up."

High above our heads, Mike kept calling Anna's name. "Annabel? Anna, if you can hear me, say *hello*. Can you say *hello* for me, Anna? Anna, we're gonna get you out of there, all right? And your mom and dad are right here. We're all right here, Anna. You don't have to be scared."

She never looked up or called out to them.

"We're lowering the harness anyway," Bryan told us.

There was nothing else to do at that point but hope that Anna would be able to do what they needed her to do.

"What if she can't?" I asked Kevin.

"We'll cross that bridge if we come to it. She can do it. She'll do it."

The harness was lowered down to her. Annabel sat for another long moment while Mike called her name, telling her over and over to take hold of the rope, and after a while, she reached out and took it. Then she looked up at him and smiled.

"Good girl, Anna! Good girl!" Mike called over his shoulder, "Okay, y'all, she is responding. She's responding."

There was a collective exhale, and I felt Kevin squeeze my shoulder.

"Okay, Anna, we need you to put one foot into that big loop. You see what I mean? Put one foot in that big loop, and then put your other foot in the other big loop, and just pull the harness up so your legs are all the way through, and it's like you're sitting in a swing, right? See how that works? Give the rope a tug, Anna, so I know you're holding on good and tight."

Anna still didn't call out to him, but she followed his instructions and got herself securely rigged in the harness with Mike encouraging and cheering her on.

"Yes! Way to go, Anna. You got it, you got it. Okay, we're going to start bringing you up, and we're taking it nice and slow."

With the Cleburne engine still a good twenty minutes away and Anna dangling in the harness thirty feet below, they began the careful process of raising her up. We waited for what seemed like an eternity.

It should have been easier, considering all the waiting we'd done in the previous years.

Annabel was in the hospital for twenty-two days after that initial surgery, and during that time, we all experienced moments of intense grief and intense gratitude. She was alive, and that came to mean everything. We knew the road would get rougher, but now we knew what to pack. That was something. A lot, actually. For a long time, that was something I'd prayed for: a handle, a set of words I could Google, any clue to the right questions.

When Annabel was strong enough to stand, the nurses told us we had to get her up and walking. Understandably, Anna wanted nothing to do with that. She'd just sustained this massive insult to her little body, and she wanted to curl up in her bed with the menagerie of stuffed animals people kept bringing her.

"Anna," Kevin said as gently and as firmly as he could, "you gotta walk for us."

"No. Daddy, I can't. Don't make me."

"I'm sorry, Anna, you have to." He stood her up on the bed and looped her arms around his neck. "I've got you, okay? We can do this."

"As long as you understand," she sighed, "there's no way I can physically do this."

He lifted her down and set her on her feet, supporting and steering her as she made the terrible trip from the bed to the door frame and back again. About eight steps each way—a huge accomplishment that we celebrated with tears in our eyes.

Cook Children's Medical Center had a lot of wonderful people on their staff, but their child life specialist, Dani Dillard, a young woman with bright eyes and an amazing smile, made a lasting, life-changing impression on Anna. Just a few days after the surgery, she tapped on the door to see if there was anything she could bring Anna.

"A couple of movies, maybe? Or some music you'd like to listen to? I have some coloring books with me. Do you like to color?"

"Yes," said Anna, "but I have *this*." She held up her right arm to show Dani the IVs in her wrist and the back of her hand.

"Oh, we can work around that, easy squeezy," said Dani. "Mom and Dad, maybe you'd like to go get some coffee while we work on our coloring for a little while."

Grateful for the opportunity to leave the room together for half an hour, Kevin and I left the two of them chatting over their coloring books, and by the time we came back, Anna announced, "Dani is my best friend at the hospital."

I was amazed at her infinite patience and the creative, drama-free ways she talked to Anna about everything that was going on, physically and emotionally.

"Do you understand what happened to your body, Anna?" she asked.

"I had a surgery," Anna said.

Using a baby doll, Dani showed Annabel what that meant and how the IV was feeding her just like her body was sucking on a straw, and why she had to keep getting out of bed to walk a little each day. Over the years, she got to know Anna's sisters and loved them as well. Dani became part of the routine that made the days and nights bearable for Anna during that long hospital stay, and beyond that, she showed Anna and her sisters an extraordinary ministry made up of small things that were enormously important to this tiny, vulnerable person and her exhausted parents.

We took Anna home to begin the next leg of her difficult journey, and the following Sunday was Easter. We sat in church together as a family for the first time in many weeks, and that was such an abundant blessing. I let the familiar songs and scripture lift my heart.

Why do you seek the living among the dead? He is not here. He is risen!

We had no choice but to accept the reality that Annabel was in for a lifetime of struggle with this thing, but we would never accept that she was at its mercy. Quality of life—not just for Anna, but also for our whole family—was a goal we would have to define and fight for. It would be a feat of engineering. And it would be worth it. There was no point seeking the full *living* of our life among the dead ideas of "normal" and "supposed to be." We would have to trust in God's grace and find a new way forward.

Kevin and I set out to learn everything we could about pediatric motility disorders while Anna relearned the simplest elements of a child's life—how to eat, how to play—

and did her best to catch up with a mountain of missed schoolwork.

From the time she was four years old, Annabel had suffered horrific pain and other symptoms. Now she was six. In the months following the catastrophic double surgery, the gastroenterologist finally homed in on the true diagnosis: pseudo-obstruction motility disorder, a rare disorder that has a profound effect on the intestines, preventing the body from receiving the nutrition it needs, and antral hypomotility disorder, which is essentially a paralysis in the stomach.

The hardest words I've ever heard and spoken: "There is no cure."

Pseudo-obstruction motility disorder in children is usually congenital, present at birth. Over time, bacterial infections and malnutrition take their toll, along with a variety of issues that directly or indirectly affect almost every part of the body. The exact cause is unknown, and it is a difficult disorder to treat. At this writing, there really isn't one treatment protocol everyone agrees on, because the diagnosis can be difficult to get to, and there's so much variation between the patients.

We were told that it becomes increasingly difficult to maintain a good quality of life for kids with pseudo-obstruction motility disorder and antral hypomotility disorder. Because chronic abdominal pain is one of the main symptoms, they're frequently not able to eat, and even when they can, they don't want to, because they've learned to associate eating with physical agony and emotional distress. In many cases, liquid nutritional supplements have to be fed through a nasogastric tube, which goes from the nose to the stomach, or a "G-button" that's been surgically placed in the abdominal wall. These effectively replace the nutrition needed for survival but place an enormous burden on a kid—as it would on anyone in a society where so much socializing and celebrating revolves around food. Sometimes it's necessary to remove part of the intestines, and surgical bypass may be considered. Sometimes a colostomy bag and other extreme measures are needed. In the most severe cases, small bowel transplantation may be considered.

A certain percentage of children with pseudo-obstruction motility disorder and antral hypomotility disorder are able to stay the course after diagnosis; they stay about the same during their lifetime, and continuing treatment keeps them on a fairly even keel. Other kids go through a lot of ups and downs with symptoms in constant flux and treatment constantly being readjusted in an effort to keep up. The overwhelming majority of children with pseudo-obstruction motility disorder and antral hypomotility disorder continue a steady downhill trajectory that has already begun by the time they're diagnosed. Their quality of life erodes as the increasing need for pain control becomes a higher priority. Nutrition via IV or PICC line allows them to survive, but not surprisingly, depression is often a major issue.

As we continued our quest to get the best help for Anna, even the most optimistic doctors agreed that there was no statistically measurable percentage of children with pseudo-obstruction motility disorder and antral hypomotility disorder who fully recovered. They simply did not see patients get well and go on to live their lives free of pain and treatment. Our best hope was to make her life as comfortable and happy as possible as the disorders continued to take their toll on her little body.

A pattern began to form. One step forward, two steps back. Sometimes three steps back. Less than six weeks later, she was back in the hospital, then home again but still pale and in pain, her little belly miserably distended. We were back where we started, only now, on the days when Anna felt only moderately lousy, we felt lucky. On the nights when there was nothing else we could do for her, Kevin tucked her into bed, saying, "Maybe you'll feel better in the morning." It felt so empty when he said it, but Anna accepted it with hopeful grace.

We considered it a triumph one afternoon when she went outside to play on the swing, but she came in just a short time later, telling me, "Mommy, I feel strange. I feel like I can't breathe right." I put her to bed with all the standard comfort measures, walking on eggshells for a few days until she rebounded and felt well enough to go back to school.

We began trekking to one specialist after another, determined to find someone who could help her. One of them started her on a drug called Reglan to spur contractions in her digestive tract. The possible side effects included muscle movement problems similar to Parkinson's disease, but it was the best available option.

"The best medication, cisapride, was taken off the market," the specialist told us. "Only a handful of physicians are

licensed to prescribe it. Gastroenterologists. And veterinarians, of course."

"Veterinarians?"

He nodded. "It's mostly used on cats, I believe."

Happily, I happened to have my very own veterinarian on
speed dial, and Kevin dove into research on the drug, but
before we had a chance to pursue it, Anna ended up in the
hospital again. This time, we opted to take her to Dallas,
where we'd already connected with a terrific specialist who
was known for breakthrough procedures—including pediatric intestinal transplants—and a wonderful motility
specialist, both of whom recognized quality of life as a priority. At this point, Annabel was on eight medications, a
pharmaceutical plate-spinning act that made it possible for
her system to function on a basic level. We didn't want to
take her to a hospital where the doctors who understood this
couldn't admit her. So off to Dallas we went.

The first day, she was processed through the ER with the
familiar refrain—chronic pain, severe distention, and a general malaise—and they ran the usual battery of invasive tests,
which located a possible obstruction. The second day, things
took an unexpected turn. An earnest young doctor came in
and sat down across from me.

"As we were reading the CT scan," he said, "we saw evidence of healing on the eighth and ninth ribs."

Completely missing his point (and now I understand that
it was very pointed, the way he said it), I started asking questions about brittle bones and even volunteered that Anna was
such a rowdy little otter when she was a preschooler, she'd

broken her arm more than once. I asked him, "Do you think this means her bones are brittle? What would cause that? Could it be related to nutrition issues that come with motility disorders?"

"It doesn't appear to be the result of an accident," he said. "In cases like this, we have no choice but to have CPS investigate."

"CPS," I echoed. "You mean . . . Child Protective Services? You're having me investigated for . . ."

He curtly confirmed that, yes, indeed, that was the deal. And then he left me there, feeling accused and infuriated and very, very frightened. But as I sat there with my ears ringing, I thought of that day Anna was out on the swing and came in saying she was having trouble breathing. I'd tucked her in with ibuprofen, a heat pack, and a good book. She never said she was in the kind of pain a person with broken ribs would be in.

"I want to know how that happens," I raged to Kevin. "How do a little girl's ribs just break like that—and how do we keep it from happening again?"

He shook his head. "I don't know. Maybe they're seeing some artifact of the distention or something to do with the nutrition deficits she's gone through."

"The only thing they want to believe is that I abused her!"

Kevin stayed with Anna while I went out for a while. She needed clean clothes, and I needed to regroup. When I came back, I was stunned to hear that the man from CPS had been there already and interviewed Kevin at length. Meanwhile, however, the radiologist took a closer look at the X-rays and determined that the fractures had not come from an outside force.

It was a relief to have the CPS issue dropped, though an apology might have been nice, but for me, the much larger issues were, first, the fact that this could happen at all and, second, the way that Anna stoically understated—or never stated at all—the actual extent of the pain she was in.

I started talking to her about it in different ways and tried to come up with some new coping methods like "blowing the pain away." With the constant injections she was subjected to in the hospital, we'd made a game out of it.

"When the needle starts to go in," I told her, "we take a *biiiiiig* breath in—and then we blow it away like *whoooo-ooshhhh!*"

It made her feel like she had power over it, and she was always excited to share this trick with other kids in the ward.

Anna saw the Dallas specialists every other week or so. In July, there was another hospital stay, during which they agreed on the official diagnosis: pseudo-obstruction motility disorder and antral hypomotility disorder.

"We are fearfully and wonderfully made," I always tell my girls, quoting the Bible. Our body does a thousand small things every moment of every day without our brain ever thinking about it, like an orchestra with all the individual instruments playing together in perfect tune. One of those things is peristalsis, which moves food through the system, but in a child with a motility disorder, that imperative neuro-muscular symphony doesn't happen. The nerves misfire as the brain attempts to send messages to the intestine, which behaves as if it's obstructed, which in turn makes the risk of actual obstruction very high.

"I'm sorry to be the one confirming the diagnosis," the specialist said. "It's likely to get worse. It's a very difficult way of life for children with this disorder. Eventually they have to go on peripheral nutrition because the body can't tolerate processing food."

Reglan was the best he could do for her, even though it left her rattling with tremors and a general jitteriness that made sitting through the school day a miserable gauntlet. On the days Anna did go to school, she couldn't wait to get home. On the days she didn't go to school, she couldn't wait for Abbie to breeze in the door with a game or a story or an adventure for whatever level of activity Anna could handle, and Adelynn was right there behind them.

Our home was a happy one, despite the bumpy road. We laughed, we teased, we went places. It was hard to commit to extracurricular activities, but we did our best to keep the girls involved and active. Abbie played softball and excelled in school. I enrolled all three girls in gymnastics.

Every six weeks or so, Anna landed in the hospital for a few days. It became a way of life. Kevin and I had the routine down to a science. Abigail and Adelynn could run the obstacle course, from grabbing backpacks to buckling seat belts to hopping out at their host home. Our friends and family got used to seeing our number pop up on their caller ID at any and all hours. They were there for us at a moment's notice, morning, noon, and night.

We were surrounded by so much love during those years, from the mountain of stuffed animals and strings of colorful cards in Anna's hospital room to the freezer full of casseroles and cookies at home. (I don't care if you're a master chef—you don't know a thing about casseroles compared to Baptist church ladies.) Pastor Scott cared for us like a gentle shepherd. Gran Jan and P Paw and the rest of the family never let us feel left out or let down. I hope the one thing Anna and her sisters remember about those years is that enormous wealth of love.

We maintained the plate-spinning act until the end of 2008. I was hauling out Christmas decorations when Anna suffered a terrifying dystonic reaction to the Reglan. As a misfired neurological response gripped muscles in her neck and back, her posture contorted horrifically. Her head cranked back impossibly. She couldn't speak or swallow. We seriously thought she was having a stroke. To this day, the girls refer to this harrowing night as "the stroky thing." In the car on the way to drop Abigail and Adelynn with the emergency child-care tag team, Abbie kept saying, "Mommy, something's really wrong. Anna, say my name! Say Abbie!" But Anna couldn't.

I ran into the ER, carrying her in my arms, and they rushed her through immediately. The doctor told her to stick out her tongue, and it lolled sideways, swollen and pale. She was treated with a mega-dose of antihistamine and released the next day. We stopped to pick up the girls on the way home, and the moment she got in the car, Abbie said, "Annabel, say my name."

"Abbie," Anna said, and the next moment she was curled up asleep with her head on Abbie's shoulder.

Looking back on the experience, she sums it up with classic Anna nonchalance: "It was very disappointing. I had saved a cracker from my Lunchables, and I was really looking forward to that." When I got home and Googled "dystonic reaction," the first website that popped up trumped her cool reaction with the understatement of the day: "Caregivers may find this alarming."

Ya think?

The plate-spinning act had come crashing down. We picked up the pieces and started building a new regimen of meds—without our big gun, Reglan—wondering how long Anna would be able to endure an endless cycle of events like this—or worse than this, because now the pediatric gastroenterologist was talking about a colostomy bag and other seriously invasive measures as the next step.

"If she were my child," the motility specialist told me, "I would take her to Boston. Dr. Nurko is the number-one guy. And he's one of the few people who could write her a prescription for cisapride."

When we got home, I got Googling straightaway and discovered that Dr. Samuel Nurko, director of the Center for Motility and Functional Gastrointestinal Disorders at Boston Children's Hospital, was also an associate professor of pediatrics at Harvard Medical School.

"She's right," I told Kevin. "It says here he's one of the world's leading physicians in the diagnosis and treatment of pseudo-obstruction motility disorder. One of his patients says on this video, 'He always does what's right, not only as a physician but as a human being.' I like that."

Cisapride, I'd learned, was voluntarily removed from the market because of potentially serious side effects, but Kevin knew enough about it to know that it could be Anna's best hope. Which meant Dr. Nurko was her best hope.

It took several months and a lot of persistent prayer to get her an appointment with him, but in January 2009, Anna and I made our first trip to Dr. Nurko's office at Boston Children's Hospital. We were both nervous, waiting in the white-and-lavender examination room with all our hopes and prayers on the line. Dr. Nurko walked in with his huge smile and jolly bedside manner, ID dangling from a bright-colored Elmo lanyard. He was positive and approachable and didn't talk down to me or to Anna. She had developed a mistrust of doctors and nurses who were condescending and dismissive, which is understandable, but she responded immediately to Dr. Nurko's easygoing style.

"Do you have any questions about that, little one?" he asked her, and of course she had many. Dr. Nurko answered them all without a whiff of arrogance or impatience.

I felt like we'd made it to base camp where Anna could regroup and find a new way forward. As Dr. Nurko examined her, he cracked jokes and asked her about her life, but his focus and precision never wavered.

"You have this condition," he told her without drama, "in which the muscles in the GI tract do not work. And when that happens, when you take food by mouth, the food doesn't go anywhere and you cannot absorb it. And as all of us know, when you cannot eat and get nutrition, then you cannot survive."

When he delivered this clear, concise description of pseudo-obstruction motility disorder, it was like a lightbulb lit up over her head. Even for me, after all I'd read and researched, after all the long-winded explanations and excuses I'd sat through, I found that nutshell explanation enormously comforting. He tamed it where others tried to beat it down. Others shook their heads; Nurko nodded.

"You're like Elmo," one of Dr. Nurko's little patients told him a while back. "You just need to paint your head red."

Anna would agree with that characterization, I think. Dr. Nurko had a wide smile and wore funny ties. His clipped Mexican accent and booming laugh stood out from all the usual bustle and chatter in the hallway, so we always knew when he was coming. His expertise brought patients to Boston from all over the world, but I had just as much appreciation for his kindness.

While Anna played, he talked with me about the risks and benefits of cisapride. On the downside, the potential side effects were very scary: cardiac arrhythmias, ventricular tachycardia, congestive heart failure. Dr. Nurko would have to closely monitor Anna personally, which meant bringing her to his office in Boston every eight weeks for blood tests, ECGs, examinations, and anything else he felt was necessary. We were told these were the drug company's stringent "compassionate use only" rules. No exceptions.

On the upside, cisapride was our best hope for restoring a balance that would allow her to eat and digest actual food and live a semi-normal life.

"The specialist in Dallas was talking about a colostomy

bag," I told him. "He wanted to implant a gastronomy button in her stomach for tube-feeding and meds."

"We should be able to avoid that," he said. "It's important for the best possible quality of life."

"Oh, I agree! I'm so glad to hear you say that. I kept trying to tell them. It's not enough to survive. She needs a chance at happiness."

"Yes, yes. Quality of life."

After a lot of soul searching and homework, Kevin and I decided to let Dr. Nurko put Anna on cisapride, even though the long-term financial and logistical commitment was about as daunting as leaping the Grand Canyon on a bicycle. The financial burden began to mount, but we never questioned that we were doing the right thing. Dr. Nurko—and cisapride—became our lifeline, making it possible for Anna to eat lunch at school, have a few bites of birthday cake, and enjoy a tiny taste of "normal."

I love seeing the bumper stickers that celebrate things like "My Kid is a Fighting Sunfish!" or "My Grandchild is on the Honor Roll!" You'll notice there is no bumper sticker that says, "My kid is living a relatively normal life a lot of the time!" But there ought to be. I know we're not the only ones who've learned to cherish a decent night's sleep, a walk in the woods, getting down on pup level for a game of tug-of-war with a happy dog. Dr. Nurko gave those things back to Anna's life. He gave Anna back to us.

In the next three years, Anna and I made twenty trips to Boston. Usually we just stayed overnight and came back, but sometimes Anna's condition was unstable enough that she had to be admitted to the hospital. We didn't want to be there, but Dr. Nurko made it sound manageable. "Now we get you better, Anna. Okay?"

After the first year, we got the fabulous news that Dr. Anees Siddiqui, who'd been mentored by Dr. Nurko, had moved to Austin and would be able to handle some of Anna's follow-up from there. The first time we saw him, he ran a test that required him to constantly check in on Anna to see how her body reacted to small amounts of food and liquid carefully given to her over the course of about twelve hours.

"Do you see anything? Can you tell anything from that?" I plagued him with questions every time he walked through the door.

"We're getting some good information," he kept assuring me.

He couldn't talk results with me while the data were still coming in, and I understood that, but on the flip side, Dr. Siddiqui understood why I had to keep asking, and he never once acted like that was a pain in his neck. He never rushed his encounters with Anna or brushed her questions aside. It was immediately apparent that the knowledge he'd gained from Dr. Nurko extended from the tummy to the person with the tummy, and beyond that to the people who love the person with the tummy.

We still had to trek to Boston periodically to maintain Anna's cisapride treatment, but in between, Dr. Siddiqui helped keep the rest of her meds in balance. They were a great team. Dr. Nurko was big and boisterously funny; Dr. Siddiqui was trim and gently good-humored. Both of them were amazingly knowledgeable and enormously kind. I guess if you think of Dr. Nurko as the top-of-the-range Range Rover of gastroenterologists, Dr. Siddiqui would be the BMW convertible.

Boston gave us another great gift too. On our very first trip, I was afraid to go there alone with Annabel, so my sister Angie gladly took time off from work and went with us. My sweet sister is all about absorbing new opportunities and experiences; if she sees a way to help, learn, grow, or just be part of the scene, she's right there. We were in the crowded hotel restaurant the night before our appointment with Dr. Nurko, all of us a little nervous, and Annabel accidently knocked over her large drink. Our busy waiter, clearly dismayed, whisked by with a few cocktail napkins from the bar and left us with the mess.

As my sister and I scrambled to scoop ice back into the glass and sop up the puddles, I heard a thick Boston accent over my shoulder.

"Oh my God, he does not have children! Clueless on how to clean up a mess."

And just like that, Angela Cimino—half blonde bombshell, half Good Samaritan—stepped into our lives with a stack of paper towels and one of the biggest hearts I've ever known. Her cheeks looked warm and wind-burned, and I could tell by her eyes that she loved to laugh. By the time the table was cleared and Anna was set up with another Sprite, we were exchanging life stories. A single mom of three, she knew a thing or two about spilled milk, and like me, she's not the type who cries about it.

Over the years, we talked a lot about faith and prayer. Angela had been raised Catholic, but church was a place she hadn't been in a long while and wasn't prepared to go anytime soon. Prayer was ... well, she'd seen a lot of prayer with mixed results. She didn't spend any time on it these days. Angela was about practical concerns—getting through the day—and at that moment, so was I. It was all the common ground we needed to become fast friends.

"Well, ya can't just set around," Angela said like a true Southie. "Ya gotta see some of what makes Boston a really great place."

Kevin was baffled when I told him how we'd taken off with this total stranger (we realized the next day we'd forgotten to mention our names!) and that this unusual person had set her own life aside for the day in order to tramp all over the city with us. Angela and Anna were kindred spirits from the off, nerd girls at heart, who were both fascinated by the Freedom Trail, especially Paul Revere's house and the Old North Church where the warning lanterns were hung. Over the next few years, Angela and her family became part of our family, and she was there for us during many of those Boston trips. She helped take us through the train system, opened her home so that we would have a place to lay our heads, and, most important, she always made Anna smile. She gave us a way to look forward to those trips, which could have been pretty gloomy occasions.

So many people have come to our rescue over the years. Kevin's parents, my parents, our siblings and friends and fellow prayer warriors. My high school classmates pooled funds and made a desperately needed contribution to Anna's medical fund. Our church provided us with a spiritual sanctuary and a powerful support network. For every medical person who failed us or judged us or just plain didn't care, there were ten others who were dedicated and compassionate and restored our faith. It's a wonder how God uses us as instruments of peace in each other's lives—if only we make ourselves available to give and to receive. Giving takes energy and commitment. Receiving takes a big ol' bucket of get-over-yourself; you've got to swallow your pride sometimes, let go of the controls, and just be grateful when somebody throws you a rope.

My heart pounded with the beating of the helicopter blades. Word came down the ladder that Anna was only a foot or two below the grotto opening now, dangling just out of Mike's reach. Anna hadn't said a word until they brought her up to that point, but now she was chatting away. Tristan and Mike were talking to her about this and that, and she was being very Anna. Calm and friendly.

"In fact, they said she was being remarkably calm," Kevin told me later. "Said it was almost eerie."

With red and amber lights flashing, the Cleburne fire engine rounded the turnoff and bounced over the field to join the other emergency vehicles. Within a minute, the Briaroaks crew had them up to speed, setting up the taller ladder and rigging the pulley that would bring Anna out into the moonlight.

High in the tree, Mike was talking to her, trying to engage her to see if she seemed coherent.

"Almost home, Anna. You're almost home."

"Okay."

"How are you doing, Annabel? You doing okay?"

"Yes, thank you."

"Anna, talk to me. Tell me ... hey, tell me what you like to watch on TV."

"I like Disney Channel."

"Disney Channel, huh? Yeah," said Mike. "My daughter watches Disney Channel, I think. I think she likes *Hannah Montana*. You like *Hannah Montana*?"

"That show was canceled about a year ago," said Anna.

"Oh. Okay. Hmm. Did you know that, Tristan? That *Hannah Montana* got canceled?"

"We like *H₂O: Just Add Water*," Anna said amiably. "It's about these three girls in Australia, and the thing is that they turn to mermaids when they contact water, and when Abbie and Adelynn and me play *H₂O* in the pool, I'm always Cleo."

"Ah. I see. Okay. Anna, I need you to be still for just a little longer. Just sit tight and don't move around. I know it's been a long time, but we're waiting for the other ladder to get in place, and then we'll swing you right out here to me. Can you hang in there just a little longer?"

"Sure."

He continued to chat to her, but for the most part, she just dangled there like a little Christmas tree ornament on a string until the pulley was finally in place above Mike's shoulder. From the ground, I watched her rise up out of the grotto and swing forward into his arms, and a sound came out of me that was part cry, part laugh, part psalm, something that meant *Annabel* and *praise God* and *thank you* all at once. There was an audible gasp from the assembled crew and other people who'd been standing there—I don't even know who was there, I was so focused on Anna. I think some neighbors saw the lights and drifted over to see what was going on. One of Kevin's partners followed him over to see why he'd left the clinic so abruptly, and he ended up staying till the end, keeping an eye on Adelynn and making sure she was safely corralled and out from under the feet of the rescuers. It seemed like the grove was full of moving shadows the whole time we were waiting, and the moment she came out into the light, it filled with applause and profoundly relieved laughter and celebration.

"Anna, we're here!" Kevin held a flashlight above our heads, shining it down on our faces so she could see us. "Mommy and Daddy are right here, Anna!"

Looking up at the stars over Mike's shoulder, she yawned, inhaling the deepest possible rush of clean night air, and then she tucked a muddy strand of hair behind her ear. That small, unfussy gesture—it's one of the moments that, for some reason, remains particularly crystalized in my mind. I felt it like the ringing of a small silver bell.

She's okay.

Chapter Seven

The moment Mike's feet were on the ground, Anna was whisked from his arms and onto a waiting trolley, and the paramedics began evaluating her. She was smiling and happy when Kevin and I ran to her, but we were afraid to hug her, and we couldn't get close enough to do more than touch her face for a moment, her leg for another moment, telling her over and over again, "We're here, Anna. We're right here. We love you."

"Daddy," she said, "I lost your headlamp. I'm sorry."

Kevin half laughed. "That's okay, baby girl, that's okay. I don't mind."

After all that waiting, all that slow, painstaking movement, it felt like a sudden tornado of activity with Anna at the eye of the storm. There were so many hands on her, stabilizing her neck and head, strapping her onto the body board, checking her vitals. Hurried feet crunched through the dry leaves and sticks, hustling the stretcher toward the waiting helicopter.

Running after them, I tried to make sense of the voices I was hearing, a blur of dialogue between radios and rushing figures in the dark field.

"Trauma center ... prepping theater ... anticipation of spinal injury ..."

"... severe abdominal distention ... could be looking at a ruptured spleen ..."

"... on our way now ... gears up in about ninety seconds ..."

"Abdomen is severely distended and hard to the touch. Anna, does this hurt when I press here?"

"Yes," she said.

"Where else does it hurt? Can you show me?"

"It's kind of ... everywhere."

As we approached the perimeter of whipping wind from the helicopter blades, someone stepped in front of us and said, "Mom and Dad. We need one of you to come with us. Just one."

We looked at each other, immediately knowing everything that was unspoken. I saw in Kevin's face that he didn't want to let Anna out of his sight—never wanted anything to take her away from him ever again—but he knew that she would want her mommy at the hospital. He saw in my face that I needed to be by her side, but it tore me apart to leave Abbie and Adelynn, who'd just been through a horribly traumatic experience of their own.

The decision was made without a word and only a moment's hesitation.

"I'll go," I said.

"Yes. Okay." Kevin nodded. "I'll meet you there."

While the flight nurse secured Anna for takeoff, the paramedic took my elbow and maneuvered me into the cockpit next to the pilot, firing instructions as he buckled me in.

"Ma'am, don't touch anything, okay? Very important. Don't touch any of the knobs or buttons or anything. When we touch down, you wait for me to come get you. Just stay put right here until we help you out, okay? Ma'am, are you understanding me?"

"Yes, sir," I said woodenly. "I understand."

"Here's your headset." He parked heavy earphones on my head, positioning the mic next to my cheek. "You'll be able to hear everything. You'll be able to hear Anna, and she'll be able to hear you if you talk to her. The nurse is right there with her." Before he closed the door, he smiled and said, "Don't worry, we'll be back on the ground before you know it."

I nodded, enveloped by noise—the jackhammering of the chopper blades, the crackle of radio traffic in the headset, the rushing of my own blood inside my head. The pilot communicated our status and ETA to the trauma center at the hospital and to the flight nurse and paramedic behind us, and they were communicating back to him. I couldn't tell who was talking when.

"... female, nine years old ..."

"We are good to go, Fort Worth."

"Approximately eighty-five pounds. Four feet, five inches. No obvious head trauma. Abdomen is distended, rigid and tender on palpation."

"Flight, we're standing by in trauma one with spinal and brain injury team."

Spinal and brain injury ...

"They have to assume the worst," Kevin had told me when the chopper set down in the field. "They have to be prepared for the worst. That doesn't mean the worst is inevitable."

I repeated that to myself now.

"Ready on the right."

"Ready on the left."

"Patient secured."

"Nose right, tail left ... Fort Worth, we are gears up."

There was a small jostle and sway as we lifted off the ground. As we rose up and the earth fell away, I looked down at Kevin standing there, one arm around Adelynn, the other around Abbie. Their faces were small and white in the wash of headlights from the emergency vehicles. Kevin's expression was etched with a grim determination I'd gotten used to. He wanted to be with Anna, but now she was in capable hands, and even if there had been room for both of us to go, one of us had to be on the ground for Adelynn and Abbie.

With my whole heart reaching out, I looked down on the retreating chaos and kept my eyes fastened on my family. Tinier and tinier. Disappearing. They were seeing Anna and me disappear the same way, receding into the stars above our house. Kevin and I had developed our MO: divide and conquer. But sometimes I felt that divide like a scalpel blade, and this was one of those times. I felt a part of myself being left behind in the dark pasture.

We'd gotten used to it, to the extent that a person can get used to losing a limb over and over again, but I wondered if Abigail and Adelynn felt it as a choice I was making, to be with Anna instead of them. Would they look back and remember only that I left them yet again? Would they be able to forgive me?

"Where's my mommy?" I heard Anna's voice in the headset. "I don't see my mommy."

"She's on board with us, Anna. Your mommy's right up here."

"Ma'am?" The pilot touched my arm and gestured to the headset. "She can hear you if you want to talk to her. Just go ahead and say something."

I understood that. And I wanted to talk to her. I wanted to say, *I'm here, baby. Mommy's here*, and my brain was screaming, *Why can't I say something? Why am I not comforting my child?*

The words just weren't there. I couldn't even force out the simple syllables of her name. I felt as frozen and distant as the crescent moon hanging on the horizon below me.

"Your mom's here, Anna. She's right up front by the pilot," the flight nurse was saying. "Annabel, don't try to turn your head, sweetie. Keep your head still."

"Why?"

"We want to make sure you don't have any broken bones in your neck, so let's just keep very still until we get to the hospital where they'll give you some X-rays and make sure everything's okay, and then we'll take the straps off."

"Okay," Anna sighed. "The lights are so pretty."

"You'll feel a little pinch here, all right, Annabel?"

"Are you giving me an IV?"

"Yup. I'm sorry."

"Oh, that's okay," Anna said amiably. "I was just curious. I've had like a million shots and IVs since I was six. Mommy showed me how to blow the pain away till it's done. Like this . . ."

"That's a good technique," the nurse said. "Sometimes people hyperventilate."

"Yeah, I picked up a few tricks. Like how to mess up the blood pressure cuff. It feels cool when you bend your arm."

"Oh, that is a good trick! But let's not do anything like that right now. I need you to stay still for me, Annabel."

The radio chatter resumed, a running dialogue between the flight nurse and the trauma center monitoring Anna's blood pressure and heart rate. Flight status and landing instructions passed between the pilot and the ground. I forced myself to focus and breathe.

This is really happening.

The Dallas–Fort Worth metropolis was a carpet of lights below us. A pattern of skyscrapers and streets emerged as we swooped in, circled low, and landed on the rooftop at Cook Children's—the one part of the medical center we'd never seen. I felt the helicopter settle. In less than a moment, a door flew open on the far side of the roof, and the trauma team poured out onto the tarmac, running with a trolley and equipment on wheeled racks. They swarmed around Anna, swiftly shifting her stretcher to the trolley.

The pilot took my headset as he delivered brusque

instructions on how to get out. A bracing rush of cold wind hit me when the paramedic opened my door, and then I was down on the tarmac, running after the doctors and nurses already hauling the trolley back toward the rooftop door.

"I'm right here, Anna! Mommy's here!"

I'd found my feet. Found my voice. The whole bizarre situation had thrown me for a moment, but now I was on familiar ground. I knew how to do hospitals. I caught up with the trauma team and stayed close by Anna's side, dropping back for only a moment as they banged through the doors into the bright lights.

"Wait! Wait!" she cried out. "What are you doing?"

A nurse wielding a pair of scissors opened the front of Anna's shirt in one swift motion. "Sweetie, we have to cut it so we can see where you're hurt."

"That's one of my favorite shirts," she groaned.

"Well, she's alert."

"Overall, she doesn't look too much worse for wear," the ER doctor said. "Jesus was with this kid today. I've never seen anyone fall headfirst from that height without serious spinal and head injuries."

"Annabel, I'm going to press on your tummy here. Does this hurt?"

"No, but is Dani here? Dani Dillard. Can you tell her I'm here?"

"Dani's not here tonight," said the nurse, "but I'm a friend of hers. Is there anything I can help you with?"

"Never mind," said Anna. There could never be a substitute for Dani.

Monitor wires and IV tubing snaked out around Anna's body. One nurse picked through the bark and debris in her hair, looking for evidence of a head injury while another assessed her neurological responses.

"Can you feel me tapping here on your knee, Annabel? Okay, good. And how about right here? And here on your ankle? Let me see you wiggle your toes, Annabel. Wiggle those toes for me."

Anna wriggled her bare feet. That was my last glimpse of her as they swept her down the hall to begin a barrage of MRI and CT scans.

Her precious, muddy toes wriggling.

On any given day, Adelynn or Abigail might or might not have shoes on. Not Anna. She was like her daddy. I almost didn't go out with him when I met him in college, because he was almost always barefoot, and I thought that was just so odd. The barefoot quarterback. Kevin was a straight arrow who loved to play football and made it sound noble when he talked about it. He had a scientist's brain and a caregiver's soul and was all about commitment to God and family. He was also great to look at. Still is. I don't hate that a bit.

Falling in love, getting married, having Abigail—it was all so easy. We were just doing what came naturally. *Be fruitful and multiply*, right? That's such a beautiful, bountiful way to express it. Sadly, it's not always as easy as it sounds. After Abbie was born, I got pregnant almost right away, but I lost the baby just short of the second trimester. I got pregnant again and lost the baby at eight weeks. Testing revealed an abnormality in my uterus. We were told we'd have no trouble getting pregnant, but our chances of carrying the baby to full term were about 50/50.

Trusting in God's good will for our little family, we tried again and had Annabel. Her entrance into the world was dynamic and unique. She was delivered by her daddy, who had delivered countless babies of just about every other species and was thrilled by the idea of bringing Annabel into the world. Things got intense when the baby presented with the cord around her neck, but it was nothing Kevin couldn't handle. I felt safe and completely loved, and our blue-eyed baby girl was born. We named her after Anna, the elderly prophetess who saw baby Jesus in the temple and recognized him as the messiah, plus *bel* for beautiful.

Two years later, when Adelynn was born, Kevin opted to let the obstetrician deliver her. With the complications of Annabel's birth, he'd had to shift into doctor mode; this time around, he wanted to enjoy it as an undiluted daddy moment.

We had our three precious girls—the family we'd hoped and prayed for—but in five years, I was pregnant five times. Each miscarriage was like an emotional and hormonal body slam. Each baby brought pure joy, but along with them came all the work and wonder of motherhood—sleep deprivation, nappies, laundry, food-throwing, and pediatrician appointments. Powering through the care and wrangling of three rambunctious tots year after year, Robo Mom came out to take care of business, and a small, struggling part of me got pushed into a dark corner.

I genuinely thought I'd processed it all at the time, and I am by nature a happy person, but while Adelynn was a toddler and preschooler, I began to experience spells of depression and anxiety. Both Kevin and I were stunned and alarmed when a major bout of depression came out of nowhere, or so it seemed, and dragged me out to sea like a riptide. We were on our way to visit Nonny in Corpus Christi, but as we traveled, I became physically sick and emotionally immobilized, which was baffling to me and scary for the girls. I'd always been the dynamic supermom; suddenly I couldn't stop shaking, couldn't think through the ingredients of the day.

Thank God for Nonny, who flipped into mega-Nonny mode and took care of me and coped with the girls during that trip. Loved me. Never judged me. Just helped me get through it. She did far more than a woman in her eighties should be expected to do; I felt wretchedly guilty and grateful. It was one of the many moments in life when I was grateful for the powerful women who surround my girls, including the matriarchs of Kevin's family: Gran Jan, Nonny, and Mimi.

Things got worse before they got better; at one point I descended into this very deep hole in my soul. I didn't want to die, but the pain and anxiety were just too much to live with—which is how I so keenly understood Annabel's desire to leave it all behind and be with Jesus. When I look back on it, trying to find some meaning in the whole experience, trying to trace its thread in the greater tapestry, all I can come up with is the idea that perhaps God was preparing me, too—

hollowing me out like the tree, lending me the open insides and homing instinct of Jonah's big fish—so that I would have the capacity to hold Anna and take her where she needed to go.

This is a very long-story-short version of it, but you probably know the rest: counseling, pharmaceuticals, and the fact that life goes on force a person to march through that shadowed valley. And there are a lot of people on that march. I wasn't alone. And if you're in that place, I just want you to know: You're not alone either.

Ultimately, while I prayed that God would give me Nonny's unstoppable energy and Mimi's unfailing love and Gran Jan's unshakable faith, I had to find my own way of mothering, my own path in life. I muddled through and went forward, hoping that my girls would see that a woman can still be energized and loving and faithful, even if she stumbles and falls once in a while. It seems that a fully lived life is going to be a bit of a roller coaster, not a flat go-cart track that just takes you around and around in a safe little circle. I want my girls to know that.

There's a wooden sign posted in the bathroom at our house, right above one that says "LOVE YOU MORE": "Life should NOT be a journey to the grave with the intention of arriving safely in an attractive and well-preserved body, but rather to skid in sideways, chocolate in one hand, martini in the other, body thoroughly used up, totally worn out, and screaming, 'WOO HOO, what a ride!'"

Mimi's passing was the end of an era, but no tragedy. When we told the girls she was gone, we knew they'd be heartbroken. We would all miss her terribly, but Mimi was such a gift to the people she loved and who loved her, she left us overwhelmed with gratitude.

"It's cause for rejoicing," I told the girls. "She lived a long, wonderful life, full of fun and love and laughter. Now she's with her savior in Heaven, singing with the angels forever and ever, and we'll meet up with her there someday."

I rather liked the idea that she was there waiting for us, preparing a great big Sunday dinner for the whole family and keeping an eye on us in the meantime.

As the lights of the helicopter disappeared into the night, Kevin stood in the field with Abbie and Adelynn. All around them, the rescuers were taking down their equipment, high-fiving and talking about going to get some food. Mike sat on the tail end of the truck with a water bottle, utterly exhausted, but he stood up and shook Kevin's hand as Kevin and the girls headed back to the house. My friend Debbie was there moments later, washing dishes with nervous energy, making sure the girls were fed and cleaned up for bed.

"I need to go check on Anna and Mommy," Kevin told them. "Y'all stay here with Debbie, and Mommy will be home when you wake up."

"I'm waiting up," Abbie said. "Tell Anna I'm waiting up."

"Me too," said Adelynn, even though she was already yawning.

Kevin didn't see a need to argue with them, even if he'd had the energy. Before he headed over to the hospital, he made sure they were calmed down and tucked in for the long wait, camped out on the couch with Debbie, and he arrived just in time to be with Anna while she went in for a full-body MRI. For the first time since this whole thing began, she was crying, not wanting to go into the small, enclosed space inside the MRI scanner.

"Can we stay with her?" I asked. "Maybe if we could be in the room."

With Kevin talking his low, comforting talk and me stroking her leg, she lay still as they rolled her into the tube. When she came out, they transferred her to a trolley bed and unstrapped her head, but one of the ER nurses stayed there, gently holding Anna's head perfectly still until all the radiology reports came back confirming that there was no spinal injury.

It was well after midnight when the ER doc called us back into the little room with the white-on-white wallpaper. The bad-news room. We had our armadillo skins on. We'd just sprung her from the hospital in Boston and were afraid to have her go back to that dark emotional state that gripped her while we were there.

The ER doc told us the one thing we weren't prepared to hear.

"Basically, she's okay," he said. "We did a complete assessment. Everything's come back normal so far. No fractures, no need for stitches. Sonogram and X-rays showed the spleen and other organs intact and unharmed. Other than a possible concussion and some superficial bumps and bruises, she doesn't appear to have been injured at all."

"But . . . how is that even possible?" I asked.

"I wish I knew. I've never seen a kid fall from a third-floor height and not sustain at least a couple of broken bones. It wouldn't be surprising to see paralysis, catastrophic brain injury, even death." He opened his hands in a broad gesture. "I guess somebody up there was looking out for her."

Kevin and I exchanged a look of pure astonishment. We might have even laughed a little, I don't exactly recall.

"I hated to put her back in the MRI scanner," the doctor told us. "That can feel claustrophobic even if you haven't been trapped inside a tree for three and a half hours. But she did exceptionally well with everything. Seemed very calm and friendly. I would say she even seemed *happy*. Bright. Alert. And I notice the distention in her abdomen has almost disappeared."

This I already knew. Anna's belly had been severely distended and rigid to the touch when she was brought in. She was still suffering from the acute issues that had landed her in the hospital in Boston a matter of days before, and we were now well past time for her medication, but while the nurses and I gave her a gentle bed bath, washing the mud from her neck and combing the dirt and debris from her hair, her little tummy seemed to be deflating right before our eyes.

They wanted to keep her in for observation overnight, particularly because of the concussion. "But I feel cautiously optimistic," the doctor said. "She should be ready to go home in a few days."

He left us to our familiar hospital routine. With Anna

conked out sleeping, Kevin and I talked quietly for a little while.

"I feel like we dodged a bullet," he said. "Christy, this could have been a lot worse, and I mean a *lot* worse. The first responders were saying how you could see the dirt packed to the top of her head. She hit the ground skull-first. And a hollow tree like that—it's a whole ecosystem. What are the odds that that tree is just sitting there empty? You would expect there to be a raccoon or skunks or something in the bottom, a beehive halfway up, bats in the crevices, and down at the bottom you'd expect roaches, fire ants, scorpions, at the very least. And I know I've seen snakes out there, poisonous spiders, scorpions—"

"Yes. I get the picture."

"Imagine what would have happened if she'd fallen in there when she was out climbing around by herself. If Abbie and Adelynn hadn't been there. You know, if a kid disappears, people make all the calls and the Amber Alert goes out. The search goes on for a while, and then . . ." He made a gesture with his hands like something disappearing into thin air. "The very last place anyone would think to look for a kid would be *inside a tree*. You'd never see that kid again. No one would ever know what happened to her."

"Please." I covered my face with my hands. "Kevin, just—please. Okay? I can't even think about that right now. Everybody keeps saying Jesus was with her, and that's the image I'd rather have in my head right now."

I couldn't bear to think about all the ways this could have been torturous—or fatal—for Anna. I wasn't ready to go there at that moment. Thinking about it later, I comforted myself with the idea that Cypress and the Welcoming Committee would have been with her in the woods. They would have known. They would have communicated it to us like Lassie in *Lassie Come Home*. But I've never really been able to follow all those "could have been worse if ..." thoughts any more than I could allow myself to follow all the "might have been better if ..." thoughts when I looked back on all the pivotal moments and decisions of Anna's treatment. I had to let go of all those roads untaken—the good and the bad possibilities—and trust that God's hand was on her through all of it.

As I prepared to leave, Kevin settled in for the next shift, sitting on a plastic chair while they waited through the wee hours for a room to be assigned.

I got home at about three in the morning and crept in to check on Abbie and Adelynn before allowing Debbie to hug the stuffing out of me for a few minutes.

"They tried so hard to wait up for you," she told me, blinking sleep from her eyes. "So did I. You must be exhausted, girl."

After she left, I stood in a hot shower, weak with fatigue and from feeling overwhelmed, a litany of *thank you thank you thank you* bouncing back and forth inside my brain with a giant, inflatable ball of *what on Earth just happened?*

It felt so strange to see the neat stacks of laundry still on my bed, because it seemed like a hundred years ago that I was standing there sorting everything into the appropriate piles. I shuffled it all aside and lay down, but I didn't sleep.

My mind was already chugging through the list of things I would need to do when I got up in two hours. Get clean clothes for Kevin. Assemble a bag for Anna with books, music, her favorite hospital activities and IV-accommodating comfort-wear. Start making calls to find host homes for Abbie and Adelynn.

It was New Year's Eve, I realized. People would have plans. That might be a problem on top of how disappointed the girls would be that our own plans were off now and we wouldn't be joining the rest of the family at Nonny's. Even so, I was just as glad to be trading in the calendar and saying good-bye to 2011. Hopefully we'd be trading up.

Chapter Eight

The alarm clock jolted me from a brief doze. I don't know what I was dreaming about, but there was no time for pondering right then. Poor Kevin was still in the surgical scrubs he'd been wearing when he climbed the tree the night before. He needed to come home so he could get some sleep, and I had his truck because my ride over to the hospital was parked on the rooftop.

Feeling stiff and hungry, I pulled on clothes and padded barefoot down the hall to Adelynn's room. She was completely zonked, oblivious when I leaned down and kissed the top of her head. I went to Abbie's room and sat on the edge of her bed.

"Abbie?" I whispered, stroking her corn-silk hair. "Abigail, wake up and talk to me for a sec."

Her eyes fluttered a little, then opened wide. "Is she okay?"

"She is," I said. "She's okay. Are you okay?"

Abbie nodded.

"The Lord was watching out for her. Watching out for all of us."

"Mommy . . ."

"I know, sweet girl. I know. But it's all good now, right?"

She nodded again.

"We'll talk later," I said. "Right now, I need to go back to the hospital so Daddy can come home and get some sleep. I just didn't want you to wake up and find me gone. Adelynn's still asleep. Daddy'll be home in two shakes. Will you be all right for an hour or so?"

"Of course," Abbie said, a little indignant. She was going on twelve and had completed Red Cross certification for babysitting that summer. People were already asking me when she'd be available to start sitting for them, but I wasn't quite ready to accept that she was growing up so quickly.

"Mom." She heaved a sigh of tweenage long-suffering. "We'll be fine."

"Call me when you wake up. I'll tell Daddy to make pancakes for breakfast."

Abbie rolled her eyes and grumbled, "When you're not here, we don't eat, and he doesn't care."

"Oh, c'mon. That's not true." I bit my lip, realizing that someday we would have to buy this girl a semi-decent car to make up for all this. "Cereal with a banana is healthier for you anyway."

Abbie mumbled something affirmative and snuggled back into her blankets.

"I love you." I kissed her temple and blew a big raspberry against her cheek.

It took me about ten minutes to hastily put together bags with Kevin's change of clothes and everything Anna would need for another hospital stay. In less than an hour, I was striding down the familiar hallway at Cook Children's. When I got to the assigned room, I paused in the hallway outside the door, eavesdropping on Anna telling Kevin with great animation about her helicopter ride.

"... and what made me so mad was that the lady wouldn't let me look at the lights. She kept saying, 'Don't move your neck, because it might be broken,' and I thought, if I can move my neck, it's not broken, so I was trying to move my eyes to see the lights of the city. It was so pretty! I was so mad I couldn't see! And then we got on the roof, and they cut my shirt. The one that zipped up like a little jacket? With a sparkly butterfly on it? And I was like, *noooooo*! I wear that thing every day."

"They said you were very calm and cooperative," Kevin said. "That's what the firemen said too. They said you were very brave. I'm really proud of you, monkey."

"Well, I figured getting upset would just make the situation worse," Anna said, like Kid Cool. Her eyes lit up when she saw me at the door. "Mommy!"

"Hey, you two." I stepped in and hugged them both, bags still in my hands.

"Did you bring her clothes?" Kevin asked. "We're ready to get out of here."

"What?" I said blankly.

"We can be on the road in an hour and make it to Corpus for dinner."

"Kevin ... you can't be serious."

I set the bags on the end of the bed where Anna was already bouncing with excitement. I couldn't remember the last time I'd seen her so bright and full of energy.

"Did they say she was okay to be released?" I asked.

"Not exactly," he said, "but they can't find anything wrong with her. They're keeping her in as a precaution. Christy, there's nothing they can do for her here that we can't do for her at home. Or at Nonny's."

I just looked at him, nonplussed. "I don't know what to say."

"Say Happy New Year." He grinned. "She's okay. We're okay. Going to Nonny's like we planned—that's going to be the best thing for her. And for Abbie and Adelynn. I'll get changed and give them a call while you get Anna ready to go. They said they'd be back with the paperwork." Kevin scooped up his duffel bag and gave me a quick kiss. "Trust me. This is best for everyone."

Based on everything I'd seen in Boston and ever since, I had to agree with him. Anna's spirits had plunged when she was admitted to the hospital in Boston, and I could think of nothing more dangerous than letting her slide into that emotional swamp again—especially since she appeared to be perfectly healthy at the moment. (Another bumper sticker jubilation for parents of a chronically ill child: "My kid appears perfectly healthy at the moment!") It was hard to argue with the idea that what our family needed at that moment was a good armful of all-encompassing Nonny love.

The attending physician had to agree as well and reluctantly signed off on her release. There was simply no apparent reason to keep her, other than the textbook theory that no child could possibly walk away from this with superficial bruises and scrapes.

Anna got dressed—refusing any help from me—and she and Kevin goofed around, pretending he was springing her from prison, until the nurse came with the discharge papers.

"We don't really have any care instructions," she said. "You'll want to watch her for any neurological signs. Maybe take it fairly easy today. No tree climbing," she added wryly, tapping Anna on the nose. "Basically, she's the talk of the whole hospital. We're just amazed she's walking away from it like this. That's one Hoss of a guardian angel you got there, kiddo."

An hour later, we were on our way down I-35, heading south toward Temple and Austin. The first hour of the drive is not very picturesque in the winter. Central Texas has its own rough brand of beauty, but you have to look for it. Mostly you're seeing vast stretches of brown grass and low hills with the occasional tiny town. Abandoned farmhouses and gas stations tell you about better days gone by. Billboards tell you how many miles it is to the next Buc-ee's travel plaza, where they sell Buc-ee's Beaver Nuggets, Loco Cheese and Meat Dip, and desperately needed coffee.

We've made the six-hour drive to Nonny's so many times since she moved to Corpus Christi, the girls have their favorite stops they look forward to. I'm all about the cleanest bathrooms. They're all about the best ice-cream selection. Kevin keeps an eye open for the lowest fuel prices. There's usually a pretty festive atmosphere in the truck. We play games and sing along with the radio. This day was different.

Abbie and Adelynn were thrilled that our plan to celebrate the New Year at Nonny's was back on after all, but they were still wiped out from being up so late. Once we were on the road, they huddled into pillows and blankets and crashed out sleeping. I sat in the middle up front, because that's how we roll, Kevin and I, ever since our college days: We sit on the same side of the coffee-shop booth, and we cruise down the road like the two-headed driver in the front seat of the pickup truck.

I kept Anna up front with us. She sat by the window, quietly observing the lorries, telephone poles, and occasional tiny towns whizzing by. I rested my hand on her knee and my head on Kevin's shoulder. I didn't want to doze off, knowing how little sleep he'd had; I just wanted to sit there and listen to the rumbling diesel motor.

"Mommy?" Anna turned her head away from the window and looked up at me.

"Yes, sweet girl?"

"You know . . . I went to Heaven when I was in that tree."

"Oh?" I lifted my head, not sure how to respond. "Really?"

"Yes." She nodded, her small face very serious. "I sat in Jesus' lap."

Kevin tipped his chin in our direction, but he didn't say anything. I saw in Anna's eyes the conscious decision to confide in us. There was no drama, but she wasn't playing either. She chose her words like crayons from a box, describing some of what she had experienced while inside the tree. How the gates of Heaven are made of gold, how Jesus told her it wasn't time, that she would have to go back and couldn't see "the creatures."

When Jesus told her He would send His guardian angel, Annabel explained, "Then I started to kind of wake up in the tree, and I could hear the firemen's voices from way, way up there, yelling for me to raise my hand. And I saw an angel that looked very small—like a fairy—and it got more and more clear. And then God winked at me through the body of the angel. And what He was saying to me was, 'I'm going to leave you now, and everything is going to be okay.' And then the angel became solid again and stayed with me the entire time, shining a light so I could see. We didn't talk. We just sat together like . . . peacefully."

Anna's tone was relaxed and matter-of-fact. The flat earth of Texas rolled by over her shoulder.

"Oh, and I saw Mimi!" she said happily, as if she'd seen her in church on Sunday. "I almost didn't recognize her, but it was Mimi's face. That caught my attention. The same beautiful face from old pictures but also in my memory. And I saw a little girl in Heaven who looked exactly like you and Abbie mixed together, and I just stared at the girl thinking, I've seen that face before, and finally I asked God who that little girl was, and He said it was my sister."

135

Kevin's hand found mine. I meshed my fingers with his and squeezed, but I didn't break away from Anna's frank gaze.

She smiled up at me. I smiled at her. She returned to her quiet observation of the passing scenery beyond the passenger window. Kevin and I looked at each other, and then returned our eyes to the road ahead. Neither of us had one word to say, but Anna didn't seem to be waiting for any kind of response from us. I didn't feel tension in the cab of the pickup truck; I felt the odd combination of peace at the center of me while an electric tingle poured down my spine.

Naturally, there was the urge to feel her forehead for a fever, press her for details, pepper her with questions—or just pull her into my arms and hug her. All of that seemed equally appropriate and inappropriate at the time. The first and foremost concern, of course, was that she was showing us some indication of a head injury, but she'd just been through a full battery of MRI and CT scans that started with the assumption that she was hurt—"think zebras" turned upside down. She wasn't seriously hurt, they'd concluded. "Possibly a slight concussion," they said.

Another long stretch of Texas road went by while I sat there trying to wrap my head around what she was telling us—which was like trying to wrap my head around the literal meaning of *Annabel is in the tree.* There was not a hint of "let's pretend" in the way she put her experience out there, and she hadn't really put it out there for discussion, just as something she'd chosen to share. I didn't know quite what to make of it all, but I felt the significance of it, and I discreetly used my phone to send myself some notes. I wanted to remember exactly what she said.

Everything she said was in keeping with the beliefs we held—the Christian faith in which Anna and her sisters were raised. In the context of that faith, there was nothing strange about a little girl's prayers being answered—though not in the way any of us expected—and nothing impossible about what she was telling us.

With God all things are possible, Jesus said in the Gospel of Matthew, but isn't it our inclination to want that promise in a trial-sized box? That whole *surpasseth all understanding* thing—that's very disconcerting! Over the centuries, the Christian Church has been very good at setting up rules we can adhere to, boundaries that are clearly defined. Anna wasn't telling us she'd crossed that boundary; she was telling us the boundary does not exist. That's a lot to take in while you're rolling down the highway between the children's hospital and Buc-ee's Beaver Nuggets.

I was raised in the Southern Baptist tradition. Daddy was a deacon in the church and made sure we were there every Sunday morning and evening. We prayed sincerely, but at a safe distance. Kevin was raised within a more charismatic tradition: fundamentally the same beliefs, but a much less reserved way of expressing praise and submitting prayer requests. The good people at P Paw and Gran Jan's church had prayed over Anna a great deal. They prayed for healing, and that healing didn't come. To say our faith had been tested in the past few years—that's like saying a rope is "tested" when it's frayed to its last thread.

Kevin has gone through such an arduous journey as a husband and father—always the Breadwinner, the Promise Keeper, the Mighty Good Man. People have told him he has the patience of Job. But I think it's important to remember that Job got darn frustrated sometimes. People tried to blame him for his own troubles, saying, "Well, if your faith was strong enough, God would protect you," but that's just something people say to protect themselves—to separate themselves from other people's troubles. "If your faith is strong enough, she'll be healed." If I've heard that once, I've heard it a thousand times. The problem is, when someone tells you that, they're not asking you to put faith in the power of God; they're asking you to put faith in the power of your own faith. And I can't even begin to pretend that my mustard-seed faith measures up to the promises of God.

After Abbie and Adelynn woke up, we stopped for fuel and a bite to eat, and from there on, the trip was the jolly holiday we were accustomed to: games, songs, nonstop shenanigans, and trying to get the truck drivers to blow their air horns. Annabel tells me that she always thinks of Nonny when she hears Taylor Swift singing "Ours," because it was playing that day on the radio. Kevin cranked up the volume, and we all sang along, jamming as a family as we cruised down Ocean Drive and pulled up to Nonny's condo on the water.

This was the kind of balmy afternoon Nonny envisioned when she bought this place: palm trees lazing on a light breeze, birds wheeling in the sunshine over the Gulf of Mexico, just enough clouds to promise a spectacular sunset.

The girls couldn't wait to get their shoes off and run for the rocky shore.

"Please," I called after them, "*please*, be careful!"

Inside, Nonny was already laying out her traditional New Year's Eve feast. Everyone was happy to see us and wanted to hear the entire blow-by-blow of the wild ride that had begun less than twenty-four hours earlier. I waited until Gran Jan and I were alone in the kitchen to tell her what Anna had said to us in the truck on the way down. Gran Jan listened with wide-open eyes and a wide-open heart. She received it like a child, fully on faith, never questioning. As we continued to tell the story, privately at first and then more publicly, I don't recall anyone else ever hearing it the way she did. I will never forget that.

"When He told her that," said Gran Jan, "when He said there would be nothing wrong with her, then . . . that means she's *healed*."

Of course, Gran Jan was the one with the courage to speak the word, but I wasn't ready to hear it.

"Well, I suppose you could interpret it that way," I said, "but I was taking it more as . . . like in the immediate sense. It's amazing that she walked away from this thing, you know? Everyone—the first responders, the ER docs, the flight nurse—they all were positive she'd have some kind of spinal injury. One of them even said, 'Jesus was with her.' But, Gran Jan, let's not build her hopes up with regard to the rest."

She wouldn't be swayed. She was overjoyed, overwhelmed, praising God. I hated to be the Doubting Thomas, but I wasn't ready to go there, and neither was Kevin. We had our armadillo skins, and more important, we didn't want Anna to be set up for a crushing disappointment.

"I can't even think how that would work," he said to me that evening. "On a medical, physiological level—I'm trying to figure out what that would mean."

Sitting on a sofa in the living room, we looked out at the Gulf beyond the balcony. The kids had come in as dusk fell. I could hear the cousins laughing and playing out in the hall.

"Do you believe she really went there?" I asked.

"I believe she believes it," said Kevin. But then he squared his jaw and said, "Yes. I believe it."

"Me too."

We sat for a moment not knowing quite what to do with that.

"I guess we just let her digest the whole experience in her own way," he said.

"I agree. We just listen if she wants to talk about it again. Don't poke her for details or put any of our own ideas in her head. All that matters right now is that she's okay, and we take it one day at—"

"Anna!"

Before I even saw what he was seeing, Kevin was off the couch and out on the balcony, where Annabel was calmly strolling along the top of the railing as if it were a tightrope, three stories above the patio pavement. In less than a moment, he'd hooked his arm around her waist and swept her off the railing into a bear hug. Clutching her against his chest, he stepped inside and slid the door shut while I stood frozen in front of the sofa, breathing her name, one hand pushed against my juddering heart, the other hand covering the knot in my stomach.

Kevin set her down and gripped her shoulders, making her look him in the face.

"Anna! What . . . what the hell? What were you thinking? Why would you do that?"

"I was just playing." Anna tried to shrug and wriggle away, but he held her fast.

"Don't you ever do that again."

"Yes, sir," she said, avoiding his eyes.

"*Never*. Do you understand me?"

"Yes, I under*stand*," she said, as if she was baffled that anyone would make such a big deal about such a little thing. She said it the way Abbie and her friends had recently begun saying the word "what-*ever*" as an exasperated comeback to just about anything.

"Anna," I managed, "go get cleaned up for dinner."

Chapter Nine

We live in a rural community outside a tiny town, so a little girl getting swallowed up by a tree was pretty big news. I wasn't surprised when I started getting voice mails about it, because the night of the whole tree thing, when I called Debbie to see if she could stay with Abbie and Adelynn, she said, "I just heard something on the radio about a little girl stuck inside a tree, and I immediately thought, 'I bet it's one of the Beam girls!'"

All the local news outlets reported on the incident. A crew from a local station came over to the house and shot all kinds of film for a segment featuring our family and a couple of the Briaroaks firefighters.

"Mommy, it's on! Daddy! Annabel! Abbie! We're on right after the commercial!" Adelynn summoned us all to the TV room. She couldn't wait to see herself in living color.

"It's on!" Adelynn read the headline with great dramatic flair: "'Firefighters rescue child stuck inside a tree'!"

I pulled her onto my lap. "Is it recording? We need to record it for Gran Jan and P Paw."

"Yes! Now everybody *shush*!" Abbie snuggled close to Annabel in a big chair.

"Children have climbed these trees hundreds of times," said the reporter. The camera panned across the little grove and up, up, up into the branches of the cottonwood. "But they've never had a story like this when a giant cottonwood tree swallowed little Anna Beams."

A groan went up from the girls. "Beams? He said *Beamzzz*!"

They cut to a shot of our family just in time to show Adelynn dancing across the rug and hopping onto Kevin's lap, all decked out in her floaty mermaid princess sundress and tiara. With flip-flops. In January. That's our Adelynn.

I hadn't had time to coordinate anything in particular for anyone to wear. We just all looked like ourselves, and I kinda loved that. Abbie exuded her beautiful tweenage cool in skinny jeans, UGGs, and a yellow T-shirt with a selection of funky string bracelets. Annabel was demure and academic in a plaid school jumper and white blouse—but barefoot, of course. Kevin was fresh home from work in his ever-present surgical scrubs, and I was keeping up with everyone in mom jeans and trainers and one of those quilted cool-weather gilets (you know, the ones that look a little bit like a life jacket but are so comfy and functional, you don't want to take them off until Easter). I loved seeing us all snuggled together on the sofa: a beautiful, happy family. A happy, *healthy* family. That was the overall impression that blew my mind a little bit.

144

We were all smiling—including Anna.

In photos from the preceding three years, including pictures from the Happiest Place on Earth, Disney World, we are smiling—there's joy and laughter, for sure—but Anna's smile is wan at best, sometimes downright pained, and her eyes are underscored with dark circles. She was a naturally buoyant, happy kid, but there was always that shadow. It could be seen in those photos, and when I looked at her in that news segment, the shadow wasn't there.

"I tried to climb back outta there," said TV Anna, "but my feet slipped and I ended up going headfirst about thirty feet into the ground."

They cut to a shot of Abbie and a fireman by the tree.

"Abbie!" Adelynn clapped and laughed. "There's Abbie!"

"*Shush*, y'all!"

"Her sister Abbie still can't believe her little sister went through that hole, all the way to the base of the tree—and their mom couldn't believe it either . . ."

The segment went on with me saying something about Abbie shining her light down the tree and then cut back to the grove to show the neighbor's ladder and the hole in the tree.

"Mom and Dad tried to use their own ladder and rope, but after two hours, they finally decided to call 911, and the Briaroaks Fire Department answered the call."

"It wasn't two hours," I said. "What kinda parents would wait *two hours* to call 911?"

"The opening of the tree is like this," one of the firemen was saying, spanning his hands to show the approximate circumference of a manhole. "Certainly nothing any of us are gonna be able to go down into. None of us are gonna fit down this hole . . ."

"It took the entire department to find a solution," said the reporter. "The tree was too unstable for chainsaws and no one knew how healthy Anna might be . . ."

I have to laugh when I think about that statement from the perspective of where we are now. No one knew how healthy Anna might be? Understatement of the year, we would soon discover.

"Finally Cleburne Fire Department came in with a bigger ladder and pulley, and rescuers convinced Anna to tie her own harness."

"We were really worried about that," said the fireman. "We didn't know if she was gonna start going downhill and we'd have to do something more aggressive and immediate to get her out."

"Anna never panicked," the reporter cut in. "After blacking out at the bottom, she says she saw Heaven and knew she was safe when she saw the firefighters' rope."

"The only way I knew how to get out, what to grab ahold of," said TV Anna, "was because of my guardian angel's light."

In the real world, Kevin and I exchanged glances. We were surprised when Anna volunteered this information to the news crew, and truth be told, we had mixed feelings about them using it. We were being very circumspect about our reaction, simply listening to her without any big reaction one way or another. We didn't want her to feel pressured to embellish the story or to feel that the experience was any less meaningful as if it were just a dream.

On the flip side, we wanted her to know that we were prepared to take her at her word; no one who loved her was telling her that she was silly or crazy or that things like that just don't happen. In any case, it was immediately clear that this was a powerfully meaningful experience for her, and we wanted her to be able to sort through her feelings about it without any comments from the gallery.

"And the firefighters have a story of their own."

"We were high-fiving and all that stuff, because this is a big day for us—well, for any fire department, really, but especially for a little volunteer fire department like us."

I'd missed that part, focused on my little family as Anna and I flew away that night, but Kevin had told me about the emotional response on the ground. A lot of gruff throat-clearing, while these burly firemen shook hands with him and slapped each other on the shoulders with tears in their eyes. I say a warm prayer of thanks every time I think about them—especially Tristan, who had refused to move from his perch, and Mike, who refused to even take a break or straighten his back for the two hours or so he was at the top of the ladder holding the flashlight on Anna and painstakingly bringing her out.

"Anna was kept overnight at the hospital with a possible concussion. Once her bruises heal, she says she'll head back to the woods."

"I love to climb trees," said TV Anna, "it's just—I'm not gonna listen to Abbie anymore!"

A warm chuckle went around the TV version of our living room, but my heart sank when I saw Abbie's face at the corner of the screen. Between that little ripple of laughter and the reporter's pithy wrap-up, there was a brief glimpse of Abbie, pain evident in her face, as she shrank away from her sister, who was still the center of attention.

When I tapped on her door at bedtime, she was still upset about it.

"Abbie, she didn't mean it the way it sounded," I told her.

"Well, it sounded like I tried to hurt her on purpose—like I'm the most horrible sister in the world, or I'm just stupid, and that's what everybody's going to think, Mommy, because *it was on TV!*"

"Well, then they're also going to think I sat there twiddling my thumbs for two hours instead of calling 911. How do you think that makes me feel?"

"It's not the same," Abbie said. "You didn't actually do that. I did tell her to step in there. And she could've gotten killed."

"Yes, she could have, Abbie, but she didn't. Instead, something miraculous and strange and terrifying and possibly wonderful happened, and I'm still trying to make sense of it, but whatever it was, Abigail, it was part of God's plan. And *you* were part of that plan. You were *essential* to that plan. God chose you to play that role. Because God knows your heart, sweet girl. He knew in that place and that moment, you would be smart enough to come up with that idea to get you both down off that branch, and He knew you'd be strong enough to tell her what to do, and He knew you'd be brave enough to own up to it and come get me when things went sideways."

She blocked my hug, arms locked tight in front of her.

"Abbie . . ." I sat on the bed and lifted her feet into my lap. "I remember one time when you were a very little girl, I found you sitting on the sofa crying your eyes out—half hysterical, crying—and I said, 'Oh, baby girl! What's the matter?' And you said, 'People are dying of cancer, Mommy, and I'm doing nothing about it! I'm not helping them!' I told your aunt Angie that, and we had to laugh, because it was so cute, but then I thought, wow, this itty-bitty girl has such a big heart for others. I love that. But you can't take on everything in the world like it depends on you, Abbie, because it doesn't. I hate to break it to you, sister, but sometimes it ain't about you."

Abbie's eyes brimmed with tears. "I would never hurt her, Mommy."

"I know that, Abbie. Don't latch on to that part about her big sister said this or that. I know your heart, and so does Annabel. And Daddy and Adelynn. Who cares about anybody else? Anybody who thinks you could hurt Annabel—well, they don't know you, so nuts to 'em."

Abbie didn't say anything, but I could see the gears turning.

"It might take her a while," I told Kevin as we lay in bed that night. "She's always taken on the role of protector and caregiver to her sisters. She's always this force of light and joy and good in the middle of all the heartache and struggle. I hate that it all turned around on her—through no fault of her

149

own. It's just ... what's that old saying? 'The road to hell is paved with good intentions.'"

"Road to Heaven, in this case," he said sleepily.

"Don't joke."

"Has she said anything else to you about all that?"

"No," I said, "but I was walking by Adelynn's room earlier, and Adelynn was asking her something about it, and I heard Anna tell her, 'It was a strange and wonderful experience.' Strange and wonderful. That's what she said."

"Well. Let's just keep an eye on her," Kevin said. "See how it goes."

This was easier said than done. Anna had a lot more energy than she'd had in quite a while, and she seemed determined to test the boundaries of God's hand and my patience. I'm all for the Texas tomboy country kids, but she was pushing it with risk-taking behavior that had us genuinely concerned. First there was that horrifying moment on the balcony at Nonny's. After the holidays, on the school playground, instead of swinging on the swings, she'd climbed up and strolled along the crossbar like it was the balance beam at gymnastics. She didn't try the cottonwood tree again, but she made her way up just about every other tree on the property. I'd be in the field below, scolding and cajoling her to come down, and by the time she was finally back on solid ground, I'd be so frustrated, I didn't know whether to hug her or swat her on the backside.

We stuck to the plan, though, keeping an eye on her, listening, being available to her without nudging. Every once in a while, she'd make some oblique, offhand comment—

like that "strange and wonderful experience" comment to Adelynn—but it was months before she brought it up with me again. One afternoon when the house was quiet and I was sitting at the computer answering e-mails, she sat down beside me. She didn't say anything, but I could feel her wanting to.

"I sure was scared when you fell down in that tree," I said without looking up. "I still think about it sometimes." I pecked away at my e-mail for another minute. "Do you still think about it? That must have been incredibly scary for you."

"It was," she said. "I was really scared, and I was wondering how they were going to get me out. I'm glad I'm a very calm person. I'm not afraid of small spaces. I'm glad of that because if I was claustrophobic—and that means you don't like small spaces—I would have maybe stressed myself out, and it would have been even harder for them to get me out."

"When you were trying to just step in the opening," I said, "why didn't you step in feet first?"

"I tried to! I tried to go in feet first, but it had just rained a few days before, so the dirt inside the tree had turned to mud. I was holding on to a piece of wood on the edge, and it snapped, and my feet went over my head, and I hit my head three times on the way down. I was really glad that I didn't break my neck."

"Me too!"

I kept typing, taking down her words now.

"When you fell," I said, "did you kind of slide down gradually or did you just go flying down?"

"I guess it was sort of in the middle. I started out sliding, and then it was like *wheeesh*—BAM! It's done."

"What was it like inside the tree? Was it all moldy and gross?"

"Muddy," said Annabel. "You could see mud going all the way up to the hole where I came in. It was wet and dirty pretty much. Not dry. I couldn't see much, but there were cracks in the wood that let in a little light. Not much. Enough light to let me know where I was and to feel around, but not enough light to see exactly where I was or how I got there or what was above. Even the light from the hole I came in through was hard to see."

"Did you hear Abigail shouting down to you?"

"I could hear her semi-well," said Anna. "Not the greatest."

"Do you remember falling asleep or passing out at any point? Passing out feels like falling asleep."

"I sorta felt like I got down to the bottom, and then I woke up and saw Abbie shining a light, so I assume I passed out. I'm not entirely sure what happened during that time period."

"Anna, you never say anything about getting really scared and crying."

"I don't think I did. I was trying to keep my cool."

I smiled at that but didn't say anything.

"I kept telling myself, 'It's okay. They are going to get you out.' I was trying to keep myself from freaking out."

"Then did it feel like you were awake the rest of the time? Or like asleep and then awake and back and forth?"

"I think there were a few times—I don't think it was on and off a lot—but I wasn't awake or asleep the whole time. It was like I woke up, went out again, then woke up, and was up the rest of the time. That's pretty much how it was."

When I caught up with what she was saying, I decided to go for it. "Anna, when you were down in there . . . and you had a vision . . . did that seem like a dream? Or did it seem like your eyes were open and you were looking at the inside of the tree and something appeared to you?"

"It seemed like I wasn't in the tree," Anna said intently, trying to puzzle through the best way to articulate it. "I knew I was awake. I was alert. And not in the tree. I knew I wasn't dreaming, because it was *real*. I could feel everything. It wasn't like I was in the tree and something appeared. It kinda was like I was taken to another place . . . and then I was brought back to the inside of the tree."

"Were you aware of Mommy and Daddy and Abigail and Adelynn at all when you were talking to Jesus?"

"I was not alert to anyone on Earth, really. I don't remember hearing anyone's voices until the end, when I was back from Heaven and inside the tree again. Hearing the firemen confused me, because I was somewhere else. It was like traveling to another place in your mind, except that it was real. Like when I'm in a deep sleep and you try to wake me up. It begins with me hearing your voice. Your voice is there at the end, but not at the beginning or middle."

"Anna," I said carefully, "remember in Boston . . . when it was just you and me there, and you said you wanted to die and see Jesus, and then you talked with the therapist? Does that have anything to do with all this? Are you still feeling like you want to die?"

"No, Mommy, I wasn't thinking about suicide or anything like that while I was in the tree. I'm not thinking about suicide now, either. Back when I said that, I was just thinking, 'Wouldn't it be great if I could be with Jesus and not be in pain anymore.' But I'm not in a lot of pain now, and I wasn't even thinking about pain when I was in the tree."

"What did Jesus look like?"

"He had a beautiful long white robe. And he had dark skin and a big beard—kinda like Santa Claus, but not really—and dark hair. And there was a sash on his robe."

"Sometimes you talk about Jesus and sometimes you talk about God."

"Well," Anna said, enjoying the opportunity to Sunday-school me, "they are both the same. Jesus is God."

"You know where the Bible talks about Jesus sitting on a throne at the right hand of God—"

"I don't know what you're talking about." She stood up and shook it off. "Now you're confusing me. Can I go play?"

"Of course." I looped her into my arms, kissed her temple, and blew a raspberry on her cheek. "I love you. Get outta here."

Anna danced out the door, and we didn't go into it again at any great length. It was just a thing. She'd said what she wanted to say about it, and I nudged her as far as I felt was comfortable.

Over the years, I've let myself imagine what she saw and heard, but I haven't let my curiosity or spiritual longing get the better of me. The experience belongs to Anna, and for now, she's chosen to keep it close. Needless to say, I'm burning with curiosity, and I'm sure others are as well. But first and foremost, I want what's best for Anna, and she's still figuring out how she feels about it all. Pondering it in her heart. I won't take that away from her.

After coming up with any number of parables and possibilities, trying to make his disciples understand the concept of God's home base—many mansions, wedding feasts, wheat fields—Jesus finally flat-out told them: *The kingdom of God is within you*. For all our curiosity, our craving to know what Heaven is like, maybe in the stillness of our own hearts, if we ever quieten down enough to listen, we already know. I haven't seen it with my eyes, but I know as surely as I know the wind is in the trees that it's a place of utter love, absolute peace, and eternal joy. Once I'd seen it through my daughter's eyes, I could see shimmering slivers of it in the world around me.

"I heard Annabel took a tumble and had to be rescued by the fire department."

It didn't surprise me at all when I started hearing from some of the other mothers at school. Teachers and classmates of all three girls had seen the news coverage, and while Annabel is the type of person who'd rather go with the flow than be in the limelight, she wasn't about to deny it when other kids challenged her about saying she went to Heaven and saw Jesus. Abbie was, as always, Annabel's staunchest defender, and now she was a regular apostle, spreading the good news of this amazing miracle in which she had played a key role in God's plan. Meanwhile, Adelynn—well, she is the one who would rather be in the limelight. A big limelight. With roses being strewn at her feet. That's our Adelynn. As is often the case, the playground was a microcosm of the world around it, and we live on the giant silver buckle of the Bible Belt, so the response was overwhelmingly positive.

After I'd gotten more than a few phone calls about it, I asked Anna after school one day if anyone was bothering her or making her feel uncomfortable. She couldn't wriggle away fast enough.

"It's fine, Mommy. I just answer their questions. I don't mind talking about it."

I caught Abbie on her way outside to her favorite reading spot and asked her the same question.

"Mom, she tells the story the same way every time. It doesn't change. And you should see the look on her face. They just see the honesty and how she comes alive when she talks about it, and then they know there's no way this little girl is making this up. And the way she speaks ... just the other day, she said she wanted to tell me more about it and I asked her what it was like when she was 'floating,' and she said, 'It was like being suspended above the universe.' That's so not a nine-year-old thing to say. But it's totally Annabel."

Functioning out in the pragmatic and down-to-earth world of rural Joshua County, Kevin caught his share of fallout from the news coverage, but most of it was people asking him,

"When are you gonna cut down that tree?" He didn't have an answer. In fact, he was struggling with it, and so was I. Of course, the girls' safety was our number-one concern, but clearly they were not about to go climbing up there again, and just in case their curiosity overcame their better judgment, Kevin had immediately trimmed away the saplings and low branches that made it possible for them to shinny up there.

None of us looked at the tree as an enemy. Staring up at the ceiling at night, I thought about some of the dark places we'd dropped into during our life together. Now the tree seemed to express what we'd been through better than any words I could come up with. In my mind, it became a metaphor for how isolated Anna was by her illness and how desperately we'd tried to save her. It gave me a new way to think about my own struggle with depression, which feels a lot like being dropped into a deep, dark hole that you can't claw your way out of. The people who love you are right close by—oh, they could reach out and touch you, and they *want* to, they are desperate to get to you—but you're locked inside this impenetrable shell, and it seems like there's no light, no air, no way out that you can see, and so you just curl up into a little ball and sit there. There's no way your loved ones can know what's really happening to you, and there's no way you can ever understand what hell they're going through as they struggle to save you.

Getting someone out of that hole takes a team: technical expertise, faith, love, and a lot of patience. It was a place I never could have completely gotten out of on my own.

Thank God that Kevin is incapable of giving up on me. He is a realist who named his daughter Faith.

Most people kidded or questioned him about the tree, but he told me later that there was one client at the clinic who is an atheist and heard about Anna's rescue and brought it up with him on her next visit.

"So tell me, Dr. Beam, how do you respond to people who don't believe like you do? I can't be the only one who's a little skeptical about the idea that a little girl fell into a hollow tree and met up with Jesus. I mean, c'mon. You're a doctor. You're a scientist. You know how this could be explained."

"Honestly," he said, "I can't explain what happened to her physically while she was in that tree—and I've given it a lot of thought. I wasn't there, so all I have to go on is the radiological data and the medical records from before and after. The proof is in the pudding. She wasn't well before. Now she is. Those are the only facts I have. All I know beyond that is that she believes she went to Heaven. And I believe her when she tells me she believes it."

The proof is in the pudding, we kept saying, because we didn't want to say anything else. The idea that Anna was truly and completely healed was too dangerous to even contemplate. She was well, but we couldn't ignore the reality that pseudo-obstruction motility disorder has no cure; the best we'd been told to hope for was a reasonable quality of life if we were able to find that balance with the right barrage of medications, continual constant care, periods of going without eating, and surgery when necessary. If we were to start chiming the church bells about how our daughter was healed and then she relapsed, she'd be crushed. The faith of anyone who believed it—including Abbie and Adelynn—would be crushed.

Beyond that, we felt like we'd jinx it or something by even talking about it.

When one of us noticed that Anna's tummy remained flat or that another week had gone by with no complaints or requests for pain relief, we'd look at each other, hoping and waiting, unwilling to say the word.

"Watch and wait," Kevin said, and Lord knows I was familiar with the phrase. We'd done a prodigious amount of watching and waiting since Anna was four and began presenting with the first serious symptoms of the disorder. From the time she was in preschool, not surprisingly, the school nurse and I had been in contact on a weekly, sometimes daily, basis.

When I saw her number pop up on my phone sometime around Valentine's Day, I realized I hadn't heard from her in the weeks since school had started again in January.

"I just saw Annabel in the hallway," she said. "I told her 'I've missed you!' She was so sweet and funny. Gave me a big hug and told me all about her big adventure over Christmas break. Christy, I can't believe how much better she is since school let out for the holidays. I just wanted to give you a call and let you know I'm so happy to see her doing so well."

When Annabel got home, I asked her, "How's your tummy, sweet girl?"

"It hurts," she said, and nestled into my lap on a kitchen chair. But a few minutes later, she was raring to go, bare-footin' it out the door.

"She says her stomach hurts," I told Kevin later that night, "but she never asks for pain meds. In fact, now that I think about it, she hasn't asked for anything since . . ."

I couldn't finish the sentence, and Kevin didn't finish it for me.

"How often does she complain that it's hurting?" he asked.

"Pretty much only when I ask her. If I don't mention it, she doesn't seem to have any problem."

He considered it for a moment and said, "Maybe it's because normal kids pretend they have a stomachache when they need a little extra attention or don't want to do their homework."

In effect, he was saying, *Think horses, not zebras.* And I was so used to thinking zebras, I didn't even know the horse when it trotted into the kitchen looking for an extra hug. I know this sounds strange—and I'm certainly not com-plaining—but it wasn't easy adjusting to the idea that Anna's health issues weren't the most pressing item on the agenda. She was still on a range of medications, but the daily coping and coddling were suddenly displaced by less dramatic concerns like spelling tests and mathematics homework.

Anna had spent more than sixty days in the hospital and countless more convalescing at home on the couch, not to mention the half days or full days she'd spent in waiting rooms and doctors' surgeries or the nurse's office at school.

She had a lot of catching up to do, and she was feeling well enough to do it. We hooked her up with a tutoring program and took her in every day after school. This didn't go down well initially, and for the first time in her life, we actually saw Anna exaggerating rather than minimizing phantom tummy aches. And so we proudly earned yet another bumper sticker nobody wants on their car: "My kid is *pretending* to have a tummy ache!"

We were in constant contact with her teachers, who were nothing short of astonished at the change in her—not just physically, but also academically, emotionally, and socially. Dr. Siddiqui had noted on her chart when he first started seeing her that Annabel tended to use baby talk—a common coping mechanism in children who are chronically ill, which is traumatic and casts them in a terrifyingly vulnerable position. Kevin and I did notice that her speech wasn't at the level Abbie's had been at her age, but Abbie was always way ahead of other kids her age, so we weren't super concerned.

Now her speech began to improve, and I don't just mean diction. She was communicating and socializing with a whole new spirit, really engaging with kids in her class and at church in a way she never could before. Chronic illness can be terribly isolating for an adult, but it's a thousand times worse for a little kid who's just figuring out how to interact with others.

By the end of February, the dramatic change in Anna was undeniable. For a long time, she'd been on a rotating regimen of antibiotics, two weeks on, two weeks off. When it was time for her to start a new course, I called Dr. Siddiqui and said, "Annabel is remarkably better. Can we skip this round of antibiotics and see how it goes?"

As the words came out of my mouth, I felt a rush of gratitude.

Annabel is remarkably better.

I looked at the complicated spreadsheet that mapped out the times and dosages for her medications. Some were given on a regular schedule. Others, like the painkillers, were given as needed. For years, everything about my day revolved around the schedule for her medication and nutrition needs, which I had timed almost to the minute, including a dose that had to be administered every four hours, even at night—and many nights we'd be getting up to administer pain relievers or just sit with her while she suffered.

Now the every-four-hours medication was scaled back to every five and then every six hours. Instead of ten different medications every day, she was now taking three. And the stipulation "as needed" had dwindled to mean "not at all." Annabel was keeping up with her schoolwork and—more challenging—keeping up with Adelynn and Abigail, tearing around the property, climbing, jumping, running, swinging. And Kevin and I were sleeping for six blessed, luxurious, uninterrupted hours every night.

We were nervous about the continuing step-down with the cisapride. That was our big gun, the very scary but very effective drug that had restored some semblance of normalcy to Anna's life.

During the previous two years, when she wasn't on cisapride, she hadn't been able to eat at all. Liquid diet only, which left her cranky and unsatisfied and feeling wretchedly left out and dysfunctional during family meals and school lunches. When she was on cisapride, she could eat soft, bland foods like chicken soup, cream crackers, and jelly. Not much better. The first thing doctors did whenever there was a flare-up was take away her food. When she was in the hospital, she was fed with peripheral nutrition through IVs or the PICC line until she could be slowly transitioned to liquids with hopes of graduating to real food. She felt singled out and punished when other kids in the class got a Halloween cupcake or when she attended a birthday party where tacos and crisps were on the menu.

We held our breath the first time we saw her eating pizza with Adelynn and Abbie two hours after skipping her cisapride. The first time she was actually able to eat a McDonald's Happy Meal, we celebrated like she'd sunk the Spanish Armada.

The whole time Anna was on cisapride, we had to take her to Boston as often as every four to six weeks to see Dr. Nurko, but when the time came for her February appointment, we decided to cancel. He and Dr. Siddiqui were always in contact, and with their blessing, we took Anna off the cisapride, which meant there was really no pressing urgency for Dr. Nurko to see her. Six more weeks went by, and we canceled again, because by this time, Anna appeared to be as healthy as any other kid on the playground. Dr. Siddiqui and Dr. Moses, the pediatrician, were over the moon about the progress she'd made. But canceling that next appointment with Dr. Nurko—Anna's powerful advocate and friend—was huge. We were beginning to get comfortable with the idea that Anna was well, but the stakes were so high, and Anna's hopes had been dashed so many times before. Kevin and I thought and prayed on it long and hard. It was thrilling and terrifying to let go of our life raft and drop that last dose of cisapride into the trash.

Cisapride was the big one. The potential side effects were serious, including long-term damage to her heart. Anyone taking this drug had to be closely monitored on a continual basis, so Anna had to have an ECG every six weeks. Blood analysis every four to six weeks kept track of what the drug, in combination with all the other drugs she was on, was doing to her system in general. It was a risk, but it was worth the chance at a semi-normal life.

Now she was free of it. For the moment. But we still had all those other meds lined up on the pantry shelf. The antibiotics she took twice a day as part of a concerted effort to keep her out of the hospital and free of bacterial infections that could tip the balance against her. But taking all those antibiotics has an effect on the system, too, so she had to do two weeks on, two weeks off, rotating different types of antibiotics so she wouldn't develop a resistance, always looking for signs that her digestive system had slowed to a crawl or shut down completely. Good bacteria had to be ingested, because they were being eliminated along with the bad bacteria. The nerve damage in her intestines was addressed with a hefty four-times-a-day anticonvulsant, which protected her from constantly gripping pain. She took prescription-strength laxatives and reflux medication, another anticonvulsant for cramping, prescription painkillers as needed, and a rotating schedule of nutritional supplements that became more important during those periods when she wasn't able to consume any food or liquids.

Imagine paddling a canoe with your little daughter next to you, and the canoe is piled high with everything she needs to stay alive. We did not want to tip this canoe. It had taken us so long to get to this balance. But now, everything had changed. It was terrifying and thrilling at the same time. We carefully weighed each decision as we very gingerly eased her off each medication.

"Okay," I'd say. "We seem to be doing all right without that."

"I agree," Kevin would say. And finally one evening, he went so far as to say, "She seems to be doing really great in general. Do you think maybe she really is—"

"Don't say it." I held up my hand. "Let's just ... be here."

He nodded. "I agree."

We watched. We waited, not expecting the other shoe to drop but wanting to be emotionally prepared to handle it— and help Anna handle it—if it did.

Oh, ye of little faith.

Remember the story about Doubting Thomas? Jesus returned to His disciples after He was crucified and had risen again, but ol' Thomas, he just wasn't going to be that easygoing about it. He wanted to touch the wounds on Jesus' body and hands. He wanted to see some scientific evidence that, yeah, this is really happening. Jesus wasn't mad about it at all. I love that response—*oh, ye of little faith*—and I hear Him saying it with a smile, a sigh, because He knew that this lack of faith came from a place of having been disappointed before and a place of loving Jesus and wanting it so dearly to be true.

"You're right," said Kevin. "I don't want to say it out loud either, but ... you know what's weird?"

"Weird—compared to getting swallowed by a tree?"

"Well, there's that," he laughed, "but I was just thinking it was easier somehow when we were tracking all the things that were going wrong. We could write on a chart what meds she was taking. We could mark on the calendar whether or not she was able to go to school, what she ate, and what her temperature was."

"But now we're trying to track things that *aren't* happening."

"Right," Kevin said. "And that's more of a challenge, sci-entifically speaking. Empirical evidence is about showing that something exists. It's a lot harder to prove that some-thing doesn't exist."

He was absolutely right. Ask Doubting Thomas.

By the end of the school year, Anna had blossomed like a little tiger lily and was thriving in all the ways you hope your child will thrive. Her grades were up. She had friends. She had fun. She made plans. She stayed up late reading and invited friends for sleepovers. Kevin and I were able to host all the people who'd helped us over the years for backyard barbecues and be the ones volunteering to help someone else with childcare for a change. Kevin joined the teaching rotation for Homebuilders, a Sunday evening Bible study, and from then on, every other week, the whole group came for dinner at our place. It was such a joy to serve our happily extended family. Feeding our people the way they fed us felt like a great privilege.

One of the sweetest aspects of all this was how happy it made Abbie and Adelynn. The Beam sisters were a trio, as God intended them to be.

I loved seeing them at gymnastics together. I'd enrolled them the year before, just as a way to get Anna out there and involved in some kind of movement, and Abbie and Adelynn loved it, but it was hard to keep it up with the financial stress we were facing. We were able to attend so rarely, it ended up being more of a frustration than a help.

But this year, Anna was the one pushing everyone to hurry, hurry, hurry out the door so we wouldn't be late for gymnastics. She had big plans for a gymnastics-themed party for her tenth birthday. Tearing around the place, she kept up with her friends and sisters, bouncing and balancing. The year before, her little leotard had stretched thin and uncomfortable across her distended belly. Now she looked just as healthy and normal as all the other little girls.

That summer, instead of remaining cloistered, pale and in pain, watching *H₂O: Just Add Water* on TV, Anna was out in the swimming pool with her sisters, three sun-screened mermaids splashing and laughing until the sun went down. When Kevin walked in the door at the end of the day and roused everyone out for a trip to Pirates Cove, they didn't have to beg and cajole Anna to come with them—or worse yet, leave her behind feeling left out and blue. For the first time in years, my attention was evenly divided between my three little fish, and some days, I actually had a little time for myself. I hardly knew what to do with that.

That summer went by like summers are supposed to—in a blur of bike rides and laughter and trips to the farmers' market—but beyond that, there was an intensely joyful aura about it. Autumn came and went with all the back-to-school hustle. We ventured to sign up for a full round of extra-curricular activities the girls had always begged to be involved in. It was always so hard to make a commitment to anything, knowing that Anna would miss out 75 percent of the time and Abbie and Adelynn would be forced to sit out as well unless I made a part-time job of calling around to find them rides.

Now we were all on board and busy. Anna was on track with her schoolwork from day one and never fell behind again. That alone lifted a veil of stress that I hadn't even fully recognized before. We had bigger fish to fry. Now we were frying the same fish as any other happy, healthy, overscheduled family.

In what seemed like the blink of an eye, it was December, and I started decorating for Christmas. We never start before December 2, because that's Adelynn's birthday, and I never wanted her special day to be overwhelmed by holiday doings. We make sure it's set apart as a wonderful day all its own, and then we kick off the festivities.

As I unload box after box of family keepsakes, the girls

hunt for their favorite treasures. Just about every single item has some special memory from years gone by. One of the favorites from when they were little was a Disney princess village, but by this time there were only a couple of dolls and houses left of it. Those Disney princesses saw a lot of action over the years, so most of it ended up broken, but the Beam princesses were unwilling to let go of the few remaining pieces. The Santa collection is my thing, so they let me handle that myself, and I organize all the items according to size and function, getting everything laid out on the dining room table.

Of course, the big thing is the tree. Our Christmas tree isn't one of those carefully chosen and festooned theme trees—quite the opposite. It's an eclectic tree filled with memories, a living, changing reminder of where we came from and how we've grown and changed as a family. There are lots of mementos from Gran Jan and Nonny. Every year, ever since I was part of the family, they would send each one of us something special right after Thanksgiving—a carefully chosen ornament specifically for that person—just to get the ball rolling and let us know they're as excited about Christmas as the kids are.

The girls are endlessly fascinated by the ornaments Kevin and I made when we were little children, and I'm endlessly fascinated by the ornaments they made when they were little. They love hearing Kevin tell the stories behind all the odds and ends that were given to us as gifts. Of course, there's a heated discussion about the star: who put it up last year, who gets to put it up this year, why someone else is clearly not as well suited for this task. Ultimately, it's Kevin's call, and the lucky winner is lifted up into the air, and the star is placed with a lot of excitement and singing. Then it's time for cocoa and popcorn with Christmas carols playing through the TV.

While Kevin and the girls admire the tree, I just take it all in. The lights. The fragrance. The joy. Even during the tough times, we're able to find hope and joy at Christmas. We didn't have to work hard to find joy and hope that year. Anna was happily horsing around with her sisters, drinking cocoa and eating popcorn. As I continued to bustle around getting things done, Kevin would catch my hand every once in a while, and we'd offer each other a secret smile. But we still weren't ready to say it out loud.

The week after the tree went up, I took Anna in for a scheduled appointment with Dr. Siddiqui. She knew the drill and stretched out on the examination table. He put his hands under the paper gown and pressed firmly around the bottom of her rib cage and across her belly.

"Does this hurt? How about here? This? No?"

It was a stark contrast to previous appointments, especially when she was very little and the palpation was incredibly painful, and she couldn't understand why she had to be hurt like that. As Dr. Siddiqui prodded and pushed at the structure of her digestive tract, she chatted happily with him about all our plans for Christmas and what she was doing in school.

"This doesn't hurt you?" he interrupted. She shook her head, and he pushed harder. "How about this? And this? No pain here at all?"

The look on his face was what I had been waiting for, I think.

In Hebrews, Paul wrote, *Now faith is the substance of things hoped for, the evidence of things not seen.*

This was the evidence we'd been waiting for.

By Christmas 2012, Annabel wasn't just maintaining a balance; she was recovering from both the disorder and the brutal side effects of the treatments. None of her doctors ever suggested that she could have been misdiagnosed initially. In fact, we were told that she presented as a textbook case of antral hypomotility disorder and pseudo-obstruction motility disorder. That never changed once she was diagnosed. She'd been seen by both her pediatrician and Dr. Siddiqui, and they were thrilled with her progress but were at a loss to explain what was happening to her. They actively discouraged use of the word *cured*, however.

"No one is *ever* cured of these disorders," we were told.

Kevin and I tentatively settled on the word *well*; it was the meaning of the word that mattered anyway, and to us *well* meant in this moment, on this day, she is in good health. We were willing to trust that God's hand would be in whatever came our way the next day or the next moment.

We were about to mark a full year without a single visit to the emergency room, not a single frantic call to the doctor, not a day away from school with debilitating gastrointestinal issues. Along with Anna's body, our battered spirits began to mend. The deeply ingrained habits and attitudes that had protected us began to ease away. Our armadillo skins started to soften.

Anna began to let go of this terrible frenemy that had been by her side since she was four years old; yes, it had caused unimaginable pain and frustration, but it had also given her an excuse to stay home from school and watch TV. It had given her lots of attention from Mommy and Daddy, who were now able to divide their attention more evenly with her sisters.

A friend of mine who had cancer as a young woman told me that there was a weird period of grieving afterward. Everyone was saying she should get back to normal, but she had learned that there is no such thing as normal. She had to process this traumatic thing that had happened and make it part of who she was going forward.

The same was true for Anna and for Kevin and me and for Abbie and Adelynn. Each of us had been kicked in the head by this thing, and we had enough respect for that to give it the time and counseling required to give it its due.

"I miss Dani," Annabel said one day. "I wish I could still see her sometimes."

"Well, maybe we can," I said. "I think we should send her an e-mail and see if she'd like to have lunch with us. Three healthy ladies going out to lunch."

Dani was delighted to hear from us, and when we met her in the hospital cafeteria, she was blown away by the new and improved Annabel.

"I've decided," Anna told her over waffle fries, "when I grow up, I want to be a child life specialist. I would be able to help kids because I know what it's like."

"You'd be really good at that," Dani said, "and you would get to meet a lot of wonderful people."

Besides all that, how many jobs are there where you get to color all day?

We arrived at Gran Jan and P Paw's on Christmas Eve, and within minutes, the girls were out climbing the trees. A breath caught in my chest when I remembered how that had worried me the year before. What if I'd gone out and said, "Get down from there immediately," or if I'd stopped Anna a few days later when she was going out to play? I remembered her saying how they played a game. Climb the tree and save the world.

I'd written it in the journal in which I kept track of all Anna's medications, doctor's appointments, and nutrition stats. In the margins and between the lists, somewhere along the line, I'd started adding my thoughts about what was happening. My prayers. My frustrations. As Anna's health issues took less and less space, my thoughts took up more. It was as if a part of me that had been locked away was now being let out to breathe in the light of day.

I shared the journal with Gran Jan, and when she brought it back to me, she had tears in her eyes.

"I guess I never realized the true extent of it all," she said. "I mean, we tried to be there for you, and we prayed—God knows, we prayed for her and for you and Kevin."

"I know you did, Jan. And I know my parents did too. Daddy says my mom was down on her knees every day."

"I just keep thinking about . . ." She pointed to the page, drew her finger along the lines where I'd recorded the notes I hastily thumbed into my phone that day. "She says He told her, 'I have plans for you to complete on Earth that you cannot complete in Heaven. It's time for you to go back, and the firemen are going to get you out of the tree and when they do, you will be totally fine. There will be nothing wrong with you.' I knew He was saying she would be healed, and just look at her—after a whole year."

I still wasn't ready to say it myself, but I was ready to hear it now. I put my arms around Gran Jan and let Christmas come over me.

I will always think of 2012 as a year of *amazing grace*, especially when I think about where the words of that song come from. In the Gospel of John, we're told about a blind man who was healed by Jesus and went on his way rejoicing and praising God. People who knew this guy couldn't believe it. They were saying to each other, "No, that's just a guy who *looks* like the guy we used to know. It can't possibly be the same guy. How is this possible?"

And the man said, "I don't know. All I know is, I was blind. But now I see."

Kevin and I watched Anna's transformation with absolute awe. We loved it when doctors and nurses, teachers, pastors, and friends who'd known her all her life would come up to us and say, "We can't believe she's the same little girl."

We didn't ask, *How is this possible?* We just rejoiced.

Chapter Ten

It's been almost three years since Anna and I last went to Boston—two years, eleven months, and a week, to be exact—so I've lost a bit of my travel-savvy edge. I used to have this trip down to a fine art, but this time, Anna and I end up sprinting for the gate. Frankly, it feels good to have gotten rusty, to have this trip to Dr. Nurko's office be so out of the routine. It's a final follow-up Kevin and I felt we needed for a seal of approval on Anna's wellness, and we felt Anna needed it for closure as she continues to process this incredibly traumatic phase of her life.

Waiting for our flight to board, loaded up with hats, scarves, and winter coats, we have just enough time to snap a mom-and-daughter selfie I can text to Kevin and post on Facebook.

"Oh, Anna, look!" I nudge her with my elbow and show her my iPhone. "Angela posted a picture of that little pipe-cleaner bracelet you made her last time we saw her."

"What? No way!" Anna giggles.

"Way, sister. Look right here."

I remember the chill that went down my spine when Annabel said, *I made this for you so you won't forget me. Purple, because that's your favorite color, and pink, because that's my favorite color. And white is for peace.* It was clear that Anna did not expect to see this sweet friend again. At that low moment, we thought God didn't get the memo, but it turns out the memo was for us. We just didn't know it yet.

In his book *The Purpose Driven Life*, Pastor Rick Warren says, "Your greatest life messages and your most effective ministry will come out of your deepest hurts." That has been true for our family in ways we couldn't have imagined—in small ways that are intimately personal and in ever-expanding circles that take us farther and farther out into the world.

And that started with Angela and the little pipe-cleaner bracelet. She e-mailed me later and told me this:

"When I got home, I was talking to my children about Anna's health—physical and mental. My son went on a rant about how much he hated God and how unfair this all was, not just for Anna and her family, but for all the pain and suffering in the world. My daughters were quick to agree. Not knowing what to say or whose side to take, I went to bed. I lay there holding my bracelet, and I cried for the longest time. Over and over, I asked, 'What can I do for her?' Then without even thinking about it, I found myself praying. I humbly asked God for forgiveness and asked for strength and peace for Anna and her family. I felt a wave of peace come over me, and I had to believe and accept that He had a reason and a plan better than ours, so I had to just let it be . . ."

A moment of peace and prayer, from one heart to another—that's where it starts, and where it goes, we never fully know. After Anna's rescue, the Briaroaks Fire Department started training and equipping crews to anticipate tight-space rescues. I love the idea that she may have already helped save the life of someone she'll never meet, maybe someone who isn't even born yet.

In Boston, we're met at the airport as usual by Beth and Steve Harris. Their ministry to us has meant more than they'll ever know. I could go on about what godly folks they are and what prayer warriors they are, but c'mon—as much as I appreciated it whenever someone said, "I'm praying for you," it was the practical application of love that was life-changing for us in that moment. Anna was always glad to have Beth come and stay with her at the hospital so I could duck out for a quick shower or a breath of cold air. We were weary travelers, and the way they took us in makes me think of Jesus in the "upper room" the night before he was taken away to be crucified. His disciples gathered there to celebrate Passover with their Lord, but they'd walked many, many miles to get there. Before they did anything else, Jesus sat them down and washed their dirty, aching feet.

That humble, loving gesture brings tears to my eyes. I have received the love of Jesus so many times in so many small but powerful ways through people like Angela and the Cashes and Beth and Steve—who are amazed when they see

Annabel galloping down the concourse in pink jeans and a bedazzled shirt that says "Love to Smile" in big sparkly letters.

Catching up over dinner, Beth says, "Anna, I can't believe you turned twelve years old in September!"

I can't believe it myself.

Anna is a happy, healthy school kid who wants to be a child life specialist when she grows up. She's at that pivot point in a girl's life where she dreams of seeing Paris, but she still thinks that the word *chicken* is completely hilarious. We told her she could celebrate her birthday any way she wanted. She thought it over.

"How about . . ." Anna's eyes lit up. "Pool party!"

"Doable," I said.

"But not a big party. Just a few people."

As we made the short guest list, I asked her about some of the girls in her class with whom she liked to hang out individually, even though she wasn't part of their clique.

"No," she said, "that group of girls makes fun of other people and causes drama. I don't need that."

In addition to a few good friends who'd stuck by her when she was sick, Anna invited a little girl who was new in school and shy about making friends. She also wanted to include a little girl who'd been getting bullied and had never been invited to a birthday party. This little girl's mom actually called me to verify that it wasn't a cruel joke being played on her daughter. (You know what girls are capable of.)

"Oh, Lord, no," I said. "Not at all. Anna knows how it feels to be the odd one out. She just wanted to have a small group of girls who'd chill and be happy to hang out in the pool with her for the day."

That's Annabel's down-to-earth brand of ministry. You just love people, and you act on that. Today. In this moment.

That's the kind of pragmatic, service-minded ministry Kevin and I always expected to practice, so it took us a while to figure out what we were supposed to do with all this. We weren't sure we wanted to put ourselves out there when Pastor Scott asked if Kevin, Anna, and I would be willing to make a video to show to the Sunday school classes at church and then to get up and speak in front of the whole congregation. This was not long after Anna's encounter with the cottonwood, so the changes in our lives were very new, and we were still feeling vulnerable.

But when he asked us, before I could politely decline, Annabel breezed by with a cheerful, "Okay!" Didn't break stride. Didn't wonder if she'd be any good at that. Didn't twist herself into an anxiety pretzel about what to wear or how to phrase things or who might have blah-blah-blah to say about it.

"Well, how would that work?" I asked. "Would you give us the questions in advance so I could prepare?"

"Sure," he said. "But I really want you to just be yourselves. We'll keep it casual. Conversational. You know."

No, I certainly did not know. I knew no such thing. Never in my life had I considered getting up and speaking in front of . . . well, figure about 250 people, three services . . . oh, God in Heaven. That was *eight million people*. Okay, 750 people, but still!

In the end, after all the worrying, it was rather wonderful.

One night when I was grilling myself, I asked Kevin, "Do you want to go over this list of questions?"

"No," he said, flipping the page of a mystery novel he was reading. "I'll wing it."

"Don't make me smack you, Dr. Beam."

"Christy, you'll be fine. He said be ourselves. I don't know how to be someone other than myself, and I love your self. I happen to think your self is pretty fine."

Our church, like our family, was going through a major transitional period. The quaint old sanctuary had been outgrown, and the new sanctuary was in the planning phase, so worship took place in a big multipurpose space. The stage up front was set with a sofa and chair. Very casual. Conversational. While the opening songs were sung, I instructed myself to breathe in through the nose and out through the mouth. Finally, it was time for us to step up there. Abbie squeezed my hand, and Adelynn gave me an encouraging smile.

I don't remember what I said; I just told the story—where we'd been, where we were now, how we felt God's hand on us. There were moments when I heard sniffles, gruff clearing of throats, and saying some of those things out loud—especially how Anna had expressed the desire to go be with Jesus—I felt tears burning in my own eyes. I used the notes I'd typed on my phone and computer to reconstruct what Anna had told me about her experience in Heaven. I wanted to get it right. Then Kevin spoke, and he pulled it all together so beautifully with the heart of our family, I felt myself welling up again.

Apparently it went well, because after the first service, someone in the congregation got on the phone and arranged for someone to be there with a video camera at the third service. I told our story again, and then Kevin spoke.

"We've been in the exact same seat where you're sitting right now," he said, "and I've been in a lot of pain. Times can be challenging and very rough, and some of you may be in that place today. I've been out there and listened to these songs that just brought tears to my eyes, as I knew my daughter and wife were in Boston in a children's hospital, and I was here, trying to take care of the other two. We've been through hard times, and we probably will have others. Certainly you have also. The thing I have found is that the faithfulness of God has been what I can count on and rest assured upon.

"I'm a positive person. I try to say, 'Everything's going to be okay.' But I've had to allow myself times to say that it's hard, and that's okay. When you spend three weeks living in a children's hospital, you get a different perspective on life. Many times I prayed, 'Lord, I can take this. Let me have what she's dealing with, and let her be okay.' I'm sure many parents and grandparents have prayed that prayer. But God had different plans for Anna's life, for our lives, for our entire family, and for your life and your children's. God knows a lot better than letting me or you write the script.

"Very few of us get to say, 'I sat in Jesus' lap, and I'm okay.' That's something we will cherish as a family, and Anna will cherish as her personal testimony her entire life. But even without that visual representation, He is with us every single day. I was beside myself thinking, 'She's been inside this tree by herself for hours. She is going to be hysterical. What is she going to be like?' She actually came out of this experience better, knowing that God has a plan for her life, and she wants to be able to fulfill her purpose in life. That's made me rethink—maybe I do need that childlike faith a kid has. Learning something from your nine-year-old daughter can be humbling and beautiful.

"We're here in church and hear amazing messages and things, and then we go home and go about our daily life. But this is something that has had a profound influence on me. This is real. This is life. It has been hard, but it's real, and God is real. It's given me the chance to learn from my daughter, and maybe go and jump up onto Jesus' lap myself a little bit."

Kevin started to hand the wireless mic back to Pastor Scott, but Anna suddenly decided she wanted to say something too. There was a brief moment of *Oh, dear. She's bogarting the mic! She's bogarting the mic! Please, God, don't let her say anything about the time her daddy tipped his motorcycle over and swore his head off.*

"We were rock solid till that point," Kevin said to me later. "I thought, if all of a sudden Anna says she saw My Little Pony, then—kaboom. We all look ridiculous. I handed her the mic, and I'm thinking, God this is on you. If you don't stop it, then . . ."

"Then what?" I asked him.

"Then let her be God's vessel."

"I have been believing in God before I was even in

preschool," she began. "I don't hear Him every day, but I hear Him a lot. I heard Him and saw Him that day inside the tree. So I know that God is real, and I know that He has glory, 'cause if He wasn't real, I would have broken my neck when I fell in that tree. I would have died from my stomach problems 'cause I've had them since I was born. I would have not been what I am today. I'd be hurting, and I'd be dead probably, if there wasn't glory from God and if He didn't love us. He always does, and if He didn't, He would have just let me die. He wasn't going to do that. He led me to different doctors, and two or three of them actually knew how to help me. So God does care about me. And He does have glory. And He has a purpose for every single person in the world. You weren't just made for fun. You were made to be a beautiful creation. So if we all come together and we all believe in God, then I'll see you in Heaven later."

Like I said. She practices a down-to-earth brand of ministry.

A year later, Anna and I were invited to speak at a United Methodist church in Alvarado on Mother's Day. By this time, Kevin and I were certain of Anna's healing, and I was ready to claim that promise, loud and proud. But I wasn't about to do that unless it was absolutely okay with Anna and Kevin.

"I just want to get it right," I told her. "And I never want you to feel bad or uncomfortable about any of it."

"About all that stuff you wrote down, you mean?"

"Right. Anna, if there's any part of this story that maybe I didn't understand correctly ... or maybe now you remember it differently ... or if there's anything you'd just rather we didn't talk about ..." I kept pausing, trying to give her a chance to wriggle out of any or all of it, promising her no one would be mad or disappointed. "Is there anything I should say differently when I speak in church?"

"No," she said, "that's right."

"Would you like to say a closing prayer at the end?"

"Okay," she said brightly. "Sure!"

"Great." I smiled. "Maybe we should practice that part."

Annabel gave me the tweenage *whatever* eyebrow look. "Practice praying?"

"Well, there will be a lot of people there," I said. "You might feel nervous. I already feel nervous, and we're not even there yet."

"Am I still praying to God?"

"Yes."

"Then what difference does it make?"

Busted.

On Mother's Day, she got up there and prayed her little prayer—a heartfelt, unrehearsed altar call, inviting others to know the peace and love she's found with her Savior—and there was not a dry eye in the place. "Honey, I want you to know this was the best Mother's Day of my life," an elderly lady told us. Two weeks later, the girls and I were out having a pampering day, and a lady approached us to say, "Are you the Beams? You spoke in my church, and it changed my life. I just want you to know, I've been going to church all my life, but since that day, I've been looking, and I can see God's faithfulness all around me. In all the ways you said. He is faithful. And now I want to prove to Him that *I* will be faithful."

She left us sitting there amazed and humbled. I lay in bed that night thinking about it, and a thrill went through me when I thought about being a small, sparkling drop in God's great ocean of love. That peace Angela had felt as she held the pipe-cleaner bracelet, the loving kindness that includes a lonely little girl in a backyard pool party—the profound healing effect of Anna's miraculous story had begun to ripple out into the world.

Our final appointment with Dr. Nurko is scheduled for mid-morning, but Anna wakes up insanely early, excited about seeing him, excited about going to the Children's Museum later, excited about how cold it is on the streets of Boston, which are already decked out for the holidays. She's excited that the cab smells very strongly of garlic bread. She's excited about life.

Arriving a little early at Boston Children's, Anna catches sight of Dr. Nurko in the hallway, and she runs to him and throws her arms around him, squealing, "Hello!"

"Well, hello . . . Anna, my gosh!"

"You still have your Elmo lanyard," she notes happily.

"I do, yes. And look at you!" He hugs her and smiles his great, wide smile. "Amazing! I'm so glad I get to see you."

"When it's our turn," I tell Anna, steering her into the examination room.

As the nurse prepares to take Anna's vitals, she hands me

two pages listing all the medications Anna was on last time Dr. Nurko saw her.

"Could you please go over these?" she says. "I need you to review for accuracy so I can update it on the computer. Just mark the ones she's still taking."

Prevacid (lansoprazole), a proton pump inhibitor; Align/ Culturelle probiotic supplement, for digestive upset and immune support; MiraLAX (polyethylene glycol), a laxative; Periactin (cyproheptadine), an antihistamine with additional anticholinergic, antiserotonergic, and local anesthetic agents; Neurontin (gaba- pentin), a medication used as an anticonvulsant and analgesic; rifaximin, a semisynthetic antibiotic based on rifamycin; Augmentin (amoxicillin and clavulanic acid), an antibiotic for bacterial infections; tramadol hydrochloride salt for moderate to severe pain; hyoscyamine, a tropane alkaloid and secondary metabolite; Celexa (citalopram hydrobromide), a selective serotonin reuptake inhibitor . . .

"She's not on any of these," I tell the nurse, who is astonished.

Anna and I smile at each other. We look smug, no doubt about that, but I'm certain she's experiencing the same rush of gratitude I feel. We get to crow again when Dr. Nurko comes in. After proper greetings and more hugs and an uneventful palpating of Anna's belly, he glances at the unmarked list and asks, "What's she taking now?"

"Nothing."

"Amazing." He looks at her, contemplative. "Nothing at all?"

"Nothing."

He studies her for a long moment. "You look wonderful, Anna. I can't tell you how happy I am to see you so well."

It is a graduation of sorts. A commencement.

That calls for celebration. Anna and I duck into the food court at the Galleria for strawberry banana smoothies and French fries. Because she can eat French fries! We spend the afternoon with Angela, tramping the Freedom Trail and visiting Anna's favorite places. At the Boston Children's Museum, she runs circles around Angela and me, taking in all the colors and taking part in all the activities that she is just on the verge of leaving behind. I know if we bring her back here even one year from now, she'll be too grown up to experience it the way she does today. She'll wise up like Abbie has, but I hope she won't lose her joy or her simple sweetness.

"Oh, look over here!" She dodges into a corner with a big magnetic letter board and asks, "What should I make?"

"Whatever you want to tell the next person who comes along," says Angela.

Anna thinks about it and then slides the letters into place, spelling out the words *YOU MATTER*.

As we wander the exhibits, a young woman calls Anna over and asks her if she'd like to participate in a psychology study, and of course, Anna is immediately fascinated and willing. The topic is "morality"; the yes-or-no questions have to do with basic right and wrong. Is it good or bad to make cookies, steal a cookie, copy an answer on a test, give a birthday present, accept a present when you're sick? Then the questions are repeated, asking, "What would God think?"

And then the young woman asks Anna, "Do you think God is real?"

"Oh, I *know* He is!"

Anna starts telling the young woman how she knows, but the young woman quickly wraps things up.

"This is a study," she says, very sweetly but with not an inch of give. "We don't want to skew the answers."

"Oh! Okay," Anna agrees readily, and dodges away to play in front of a green screen where you can see yourself on TV. She's never felt that she has anything to prove, and she doesn't pass judgment on anyone else's views. If you're willing to be kind, you're welcome at her pool party.

There's a wonderful line in *The Song of Bernadette* by Franz Werfel: "For those who believe, no explanation is necessary. For those who do not believe, no explanation is possible."

I suspect Anna will see a lot of both in her life. She has this thing in her heart—an intensely bright "this little light of mine" shine—that she wouldn't want to keep to herself, even if she could. Abigail and Adelynn are exactly the same way.

Abbie struggled for a long time with what happened, because her greatest gifts—her heart full of mercy and her staunch sense of responsibility—worked against her in that moment. I worried briefly that it might make her doubt herself or clamp a lid down on that wildly creative and adventurous spirit, but she worked it out in classic Abbie fashion. In high school now, she excels in acting and debate and keeps her grades up, because she hopes to be a veterinarian like her daddy. I see so much of him in her. She devours books like a wood chipper. When she sees someone being bullied, she stands up and gets involved.

Kevin has taken both Abbie and Anna on long motorcycle trips across Montana, and each time, he took headsets so they could communicate as they rode. Kevin says that when he was traveling with Abbie, they burned through the eight-hour battery life of the headsets every day. When he was traveling with Anna, at the end of the day, the batteries were still strong; they'd roll on for hours without saying a word.

When it's time for Adelynn's father–daughter trek, he'll probably have to take spares. She has blossomed into an all-out theatrical diva who charms the socks off everyone she meets. Perhaps because she was shuffled around so much in her formative years, she's one of those people who fits in anywhere. She keeps the three- and four-year-olds entertained in the nursery at church and loves to "work" in the front lobby at the veterinary clinic. It terrifies and thrills me to see her engage with anyone of any age as if they were part of her family. It's hard to teach a little girl to be wary of strangers when everyone she comes in contact with is instantly a friend—from the little old cat lady at the veterinary clinic to the punk rocker in line behind us at the grocery store.

As each has received a gift, says the Bible, *use it to serve one another.*

I'm confident that each of the uniquely gifted Beam sisters will be a remarkable woman in the world, but more than that, I cherish knowing that they will always be there for each other.

*

Barefoot as usual, Annabel hops the gate and sets off down the road, but Abigail holds out her arms like a crossing guard and stops her little sisters in their tracks.

"We have just entered Narnia," she says, and they proceed with due reverence.

"I want to be the good witch," Adelynn pipes up.

"There is no good witch," says Abbie.

"Then I want to be Dorothy!"

"There is no Dorothy in Narnia. No good witch. No Dorothy. You're confusing it with the *Wizard of Oz*."

"I'll be the cowardly lion," Kevin calls from the gate.

"Daddy," says Anna, "that's the *Wizard of Oz*, and you know it. You're being silly."

"Oh, and we're all too mature for that now."

"I am," Abbie says to Annabel. "I don't know about him."

But I know. Kevin has definitely gotten his silliness back.

As I write this, 2014 is almost done. Three years have passed since our world changed. I used to say "since Anna fell" and later I started saying "since Anna was healed," but now even that has receded into a world of miracles, large and small, as countless as the stars—far more than any of us will ever know. One of the loveliest is Kevin's return to the joyful, playful, wonderfully silly daddy he was when Abbie was a baby. He still does the hard work and keeps the hard promises, but he never wanted to be the dreaded father in the "just wait till your father gets home" scenario. He wanted his children to be happy when he walked in the door. And they are.

These days, Kevin rolls up at the end of a long day and is met in the driveway by Cypress, River, Trinity, Jack, and Arnold, our most recent edition. (All the other dogs are named after rivers, but Arnold is just so *Arnold*.) Even though Kevin's been on his feet and up to his elbows all day, instead of kicking back in a recliner, he turns off the TV, shrugs off the Greek chorus of woe, and within five minutes, there's an adventure under way. He's got the girls trooping out the door and down the drive, which gives me a moment to catch up on e-mails and get dinner started.

By the time they roll on home for supper, there's always a huge story to tell, and we gather at the table, everyone talking at once. "We went hiking about three miles, and there was this road—" "Go wash those hands, please." "Yeah, a road where the bridge washed out, and tunnels under, and a culvert that follows a dry creek bed." "Anna, put some salad dressing on the table." "The road's abandoned, and people dumped some furniture back there." "Mommy, I need my other jeans washed tonight." "Within twenty steps, you're exploring Narnia." "What jeans?" "You know! The ones I like." "No cars go there anymore, so we explored." "And we danced! It was so fun."

"Shall we say grace?"

We hold hands in an unbroken circle around the table.

"Heavenly Father," Kevin says, "we thank you for this beautiful day. For these beautiful children. For this food we're about to eat. Bless it to our bodies. Let it strengthen us to do your will and be your light in the world. Amen."

"Pass the potatoes, please."

"Daddy," says Anna, "what did you watch on TV when you were a kid?"

"Not much," he says. "We were only allowed thirty minutes a day."

The Greek chorus wails at the very idea: *Nooooooo!* Oh, Gran Jan! How could she be so cruel?

Kevin says, "We liked *Dukes of Hazzard*. Luke Duke. Daisy Duke."

"Daisy Duke?" says Abbie. "Like the shorts?"

"Yeah, that's why they're called Daisy Dukes. Didn't you know that?"

"Lies!" says Adelynn. "Lies and blasphemy."

"Mommy," says Anna, "I really, really need those jeans."

And now you know everything there is to know about the elevated spiritual conversations that go on around the Beam family supper table. Believe me, it only gets worse, because this family was ruthlessly trained not to be uptight about the discussion of bodily functions. After the girls go to bed, Kevin and I will sit with a glass of wine and discuss important matters like the cooler weather coming and how astonishing it is that Christmas is just a few weeks away and what will be the budget for that, or he might tell me something about castrating bulls today. That's as philosophical as it gets most evenings.

Beyond our kitchen window, across the field, the cottonwood stands in the moonlight. The branch that formed the castle bridge gave way and crashed down to the ground one windy night when the Beam sisters were snug in their beds, but the tree itself has grown taller. The heart-shaped leaves rustle on the wind. Birds nest in the branches. Squirrels sit on the spiky lip of the decaying grotto and spy on comings and goings over on the road. We keep trying to recall if it ever blossomed before—and Kevin swears it didn't—but it does now. High, high, high in the branches, those soft white tufts bloom and let go, and the wind takes them to who knows where.

After we were in the news, people kept asking Kevin, "So, Dr. Beam, have you cut down that old cottonwood tree yet?"

Finally one day, he reluctantly went out there with a chainsaw. He took down a few of the smaller trees—the ones the girls had used to climb up to the grotto—but he couldn't bring himself to take down the cottonwood. He stood there for a while with the chainsaw in his hands, studying the dense bark and soaring branches. Then very carefully, he stepped up to the broad trunk and carved a cross. Straight and true. A symbol of both suffering and salvation.

I cried the first time I saw it, and some days I go out there to pray. It makes me feel small and awestruck and glad. It makes me think about something Anna said: "God is always there, and He has His own ways of working things out."

Could there be a greater source of peace than that simple affirmation? When life brings hardships beyond our under-standing, it's not up to us to look for the silver lining. We *are* the silver lining. We become God's well-tuned instruments of peace, His gift to one another, each of us a miracle, accord-ing to His strange and wonderful plan.

Acknowledgments

This story is my truth as I remember it. Some events and people had to be composited, and dialogue was reconstructed for narrative purposes, but I've done my best to stay true to the content of those conversations, the facts of the events, and the spirit of the relationships portrayed in this book. Others, of course, may have their own recollections or perceptions of events.

Though I learned a great deal about pseudo-obstruction motility disorder and antral hypomotility disorder on our journey, I do not consider myself a medical expert, and no part of this book should be construed or misconstrued as medical information or advice. My opinions do not necessarily reflect the opinions of Alsbury Baptist Church or any other constituencies or organizations who've hosted or will in the future host me as a speaker.

Kevin and I are more grateful than we can express to Dr. Nurko, Dr. Siddiqui, Dani Dillard, and all the wonderful caregivers who looked after Anna at Cook Children's and Boston Children's Hospital. Same goes for the amazing Briaroaks Volunteer Fire Department. We also cherish and appreciate our church family at Alsbury Baptist, my wonderful family, Kevin's wonderful family, Angela Cimino, Nina and the Cash Crew, and many other friends who stepped in to help us, feed us, and look after our girls. They are too many to mention, but each one is special in my heart, and I am deeply grateful.

Heartfelt thanks to my agent, the fabulous Nena Madonia of Dupree/Miller & Associates, who's been a tireless advocate for this book through some stormy seas. Mauro DiPreta's faith in our story and belief in this project has been life-changing for me. Huge thanks to him and everyone at Hachette.

Abigail, Annabel, and Adelynn—listen, sisters, you know that you are my heart and soul. When you read this book to your children someday, I hope you'll tell them, "Yes, my mama was a little nutty sometimes, but she loved me. Of that there is no doubt." When I praise God from whom all blessings flow, you are the best, brightest blessings a mom could ever imagine.

And to my husband, Dr. Kevin Beam . . . babe, you already know. But I plan to keep telling you for the rest of my life.

Christy Wilson Beam
Burleson, Texas

Spring, 2015